Letter Home

Investigating Fractions

Date: _____

Dear Family Member:

This unit extends your child's experiences with fractions. The class will explore fractions using rectangles drawn on dot paper and geoboards. These rectangles provide a model that helps students look for common denominators and lays the groundwork for adding and subtracting fractions.

Students also participate in the lab *A Day at the Races.* This lab allows students to compare fractions using both graphs and written numbers.

You can increase your child's understanding of fractions by asking your child to share the game *Fraction Cover-All.* The directions are in the *Student Guide.*

This unit reviews the multiplication and division facts for the nines. Use the *Triangle Flash Cards* to work on these facts with your child.

Sincerely,

_____

A sack race provides data for students to use as they learn about fractions.

Carta al hogar

Fecha: _____

Estimado miembro de familia:

Esta unidad extiende las experiencias de su hijo/a con fracciones. La clase explorará fracciones usando rectángulos dibujados en papel punteado y usando un tablero geométrico. Estos rectángulos sirven de modelo para ayudar a los estudiantes a hallar denominadores comunes y sirven de base para aprender a sumar y restar fracciones.

Los estudiantes también participarán en el laboratorio *Un día en las carreras*. Este laboratorio les da a los estudiantes la oportunidad de comparar fracciones usando tanto gráficas como números escritos.

Una carrera de sacos da datos que los estudiantes pueden usar mientras aprenden acerca de las fracciones.

Usted puede ayudar a su hijo/a a comprender mejor las fracciones pidiéndole que comparta con usted el juego *Bingo fraccionario.* Las instrucciones se encuentran en la *Guía Estudiantil.*

Esta unidad también repasa las tablas de multiplicación y división por nueve. Use las *tarjetas triangulares* para ayudar a su hijo con estas tablas.

Atentamente,

_____

A BALANCED MATHEMATICS PROGRAM INTEGRATING SCIENCE AND LANGUAGE ARTS

Unit Resource Guide
Unit 5
Investigating Fractions

THIRD EDITION

KENDALL/HUNT PUBLISHING COMPANY
4050 Westmark Drive   Dubuque, Iowa 52002

A TIMS® Curriculum
University of Illinois at Chicago

UIC The University of Illinois at Chicago

The original edition was based on work supported by the National Science Foundation under grant No. MDR 9050226 and the University of Illinois at Chicago. Any opinions, findings, and conclusions or recommendations expressed in this publication are those of the author(s) and do not necessarily reflect the views of the granting agencies.

Printed in the United States of America

1 2 3 4 5 6 7 8 9 10   11 10 09 08 07

Table of Contents

Unit 5
Investigating Fractions

Outline 2

Background 9

Observational Assessment Record 13

Daily Practice and Problems 15

Lesson 1 *Geoboard Fractions* 26

Lesson 2 *Parts and Wholes* 44

Lesson 3 *Using Dot Paper Rectangles* 56

Lesson 4 *Using Common Denominators* 67

Lesson 5 *A Day at the Races* 76

Lesson 6 *Adding Fractions with Rectangles* 97

Lesson 7 *Adding and Subtracting Fractions* 110

Lesson 8 *Shannon's Trip to School* 124

Home Practice Answer Key 129

Glossary 133

Unit 5

Outline
Investigating Fractions

Estimated Class Sessions
11-17

Unit Summary

This unit connects two important strands in the curriculum: the study of fractions and the use of data to solve problems. Students review and expand their knowledge of fraction concepts to include models for finding common denominators.

Students use rectangles on dot paper, geoboards, and pattern blocks as their primary fraction models. They then use these models to develop procedures for comparing, adding, and subtracting fractions with unlike denominators.

These concepts are further explored in the lab *A Day at the Races.* In this lab, students use the TIMS Laboratory Method and their knowledge of fractions to compare speeds by comparing ratios. The DPP for this unit reviews the multiplication and division facts for the nines.

Major Concept Focus

- representing fractions with models
- numerators and denominators
- unit whole
- fractional parts of wholes
- equivalent fractions
- common denominators
- communicating solution strategies
- multiplication and division facts: 9s
- comparing fractions
- adding fractions using models
- subtracting fractions using models
- estimating with fractions
- TIMS Laboratory Method
- measuring length
- speed and velocity
- point graphs
- best-fit lines
- using ratios
- Student Rubric: *Telling*

Pacing Suggestions

This unit extends concepts and skills developed in Unit 3 and the lab *Spreading Out* in Unit 4 Lesson 6. Students make connections among manipulatives, pictures, and symbols. This work allows them to choose among these tools to solve problems using fractions and ratios. Some students will be comfortable using symbols and others will depend on manipulatives and pictures. Most will move back and forth among the different representations. In later units, students will develop and practice paper-and-pencil procedures.

- Use the recommended session numbers for each lesson as a guide. It is not necessary to wait until students master each skill—especially paper-and-pencil procedures—as students will revisit them in later units. They also will practice them in the Daily Practice and Problems and Home Practice throughout the year. Use the Assessment Indicators as a guide for the appropriate time to assess specific skills. Assessment Indicators for all units are listed on the *Individual Assessment Record Sheet* in the Assessment section of the *Teacher Implementation Guide.*

- Collect the data for Unit 5 Lesson 5 *A Day at the Races* during science time. This laboratory investigation explores speed and velocity.

- Unit 5 Lesson 8 *Shannon's Trip to School* is an optional lesson. This series of word problems is appropriate to assign for homework.

Assessment Indicators

Use the following Assessment Indicators and the *Observational Assessment Record* that follows the Background section in this unit to assess students on key ideas.

A1. Can students represent fractions using pattern blocks and rectangles on dot paper?

A2. Can students find equivalent fractions?

A3. Can students compare and order fractions?

A4. Can students collect, organize, graph, and analyze data?

A5. Can students draw and interpret best-fit lines?

A6. Can students use ratios to solve problems?

A7. Can students measure length in yards and feet?

A8. Can students add and subtract fractions using manipulatives, pictures, or symbols?

A9. Do students demonstrate fluency with the multiplication and division facts for the 9s?

Unit Planner

	Lesson Information	Supplies	Copies/Transparencies
Lesson 1 **Geoboard Fractions** URG Pages 26–43 SG Pages 144–151 DPP A–D HP Part 1 *Estimated Class Sessions* **2-3**	**Activity** Students build rectangles on geoboards and draw rectangles on dot paper. They use the rectangles to model fractions and mixed numbers. **Math Facts** Complete DPP items B–D and begin reviewing the multiplication and division facts for the 9s. **Homework** 1. Assign the Homework section in the *Student Guide*. 2. Assign Part 1 of the Home Practice. **Assessment** Use *Questions 5–6* from the Homework section to assess students' understanding of denominators and numerators.	• 1 geoboard per student pair • rubber bands • overhead geoboard	• 4–5 copies of *Centimeter Dot Paper* URG Page 36 per student • 1 transparency of *Centimeter Dot Paper* URG Page 36
Lesson 2 **Parts and Wholes** URG Pages 44–55 SG Pages 152–156 DPP E–F HP Part 2 *Estimated Class Sessions* **1-2**	**Activity** Students work in pairs to model fractions using both pattern blocks and rectangles on dot paper. **Math Facts** Assign DPP item E. Item E reviews math facts with multiples of ten. **Homework** 1. Assign the Homework section in the *Student Guide*. 2. Assign Part 2 of the Home Practice. **Assessment** 1. Use *Question 3* in the Homework section to assess students' abilities to model fractions using rectangles on dot paper. 2. Give a short quiz to assess students' abilities to represent fractions using rectangles on dot paper as you model various fractions using overhead pattern blocks. 3. Observe students as they are working in class. Record your observations on the *Observational Assessment Record* and students' *Individual Assessment Record Sheets*.	• 1 set of pattern blocks (2–3 yellow hexagons, 6 red trapezoids, 10 green triangles, 10 blue rhombuses, 6 brown trapezoids, 12 purple triangles) per student pair • overhead pattern blocks	• 3–4 copies of *Centimeter Dot Paper* URG Page 36 per student • 1 transparency of *Centimeter Dot Paper* URG Page 36 • 1 copy of *Observational Assessment Record* URG Pages 13–14 to be used throughout this unit • 1 copy of *Individual Assessment Record Sheet* TIG Assessment section, previously copied to be used throughout the year
Lesson 3 **Using Dot Paper Rectangles** URG Pages 56–66 SG Pages 157–159 DAB Pages 77–78 DPP G–H HP Part 4	**Game and Activity** Students write fraction sentences using dot paper rectangles in the game *Fraction Cover-All*. Students then model equivalent fractions using dot paper rectangles. **Math Facts** Continue reviewing the multiplication and division facts for the 9s using *Triangle Flash Cards*. **Homework** 1. Assign the Homework section in the *Student Guide*. 2. Assign the *Equivalent Fractions on Dot Paper* Activity Pages in the *Discovery Assignment Book*. 3. Assign Part 4 of the Home Practice.	• 1 set of 6 index cards with the following fractions: $\frac{1}{2}, \frac{1}{4}, \frac{1}{3}, \frac{1}{6}, \frac{1}{12}, \frac{1}{12}$	• 3–4 copies of *Centimeter Dot Paper* URG Page 36 per student • 1 transparency of *Centimeter Dot Paper* URG Page 36

	Lesson Information	**Supplies**	**Copies/ Transparencies**

Estimated Class Sessions

1-2

Assessment
Use *Question 1* in the Homework section.

Lesson 4

Using Common Denominators

URG Pages 67–75
SG Pages 160–163

DPP I–J
HP Part 5

Estimated Class Sessions

1

Activity
Using rectangles on dot paper, students compare fractions with unlike denominators by rewriting the fractions with common denominators.

Math Facts
Complete DPP item I, which uses fact families to review the multiplication and division facts for the 9s.

Homework
1. Assign *Questions 1–12* in the Homework section on the *Using Common Denominators* Activity Pages in the *Student Guide.*
2. Assign Part 5 of the Home Practice.

Assessment
Use two or three problems from the Homework section as assessment.

	• 3–4 copies of *Centimeter Dot Paper* URG Page 36 per student
	• 1 transparency of *Centimeter Dot Paper* URG Page 36

Lesson 5

A Day at the Races

URG Pages 76–96
SG Pages 164–170

DPP K–P
HP Part 3

Estimated Class Sessions

3-4

Lab
In an experiment on speed, students compare ratios using both graphs and symbols.

Math Facts
Complete DPP items K and O, which review math facts.

Homework
1. Assign the Homework section in the *Student Guide.*
2. Assign the word problems in Lesson 8 for homework.
3. Assign Part 3 of the Home Practice.

Assessment
1. Assign points to one or more sections of the lab to determine a grade.
2. Use *Question 18* to assess students' abilities to draw a graph. Use *Questions 19–20* to assess the students' abilities to solve problems and communicate solutions.
3. Use the *Observational Assessment Record* and the Assessment Indicators to record students' skills in measuring length.

Supplies:
• 1–2 metersticks per student group
• 1–2 stopwatches per student group
• chalk or tape

Copies/Transparencies:
• 2–3 copies of *Centimeter Graph Paper* or *Half-Centimeter Graph Paper* URG Pages 89–90 per student
• 2 copies of *Three-trial Data Table* URG Page 91 per student
• 3 copies of *Five-column Data Table* URG Page 92 per student group, optional
• 1 transparency of *Centimeter Graph Paper* or *Half-Centimeter Graph Paper* URG Pages 89–90, optional
• 1 copy of *TIMS Multidimensional Rubric* TIG Assessment section

(Continued)

	Lesson Information	Supplies	Copies/Transparencies
Lesson 6 **Adding Fractions with Rectangles** URG Pages 97–109 SG Pages 82, 171–176 DPP Q–T *Estimated Class Sessions* **2**	**Activity** Students estimate sums of fractions using 0, $\frac{1}{2}$, and 1 as benchmarks. Then, they use rectangles on dot paper to develop and use procedures for adding fractions. **Math Facts** Complete DPP item S, which is a quiz on the facts. **Homework** 1. You may assign *Questions 15–25* in the Explore section for homework. 2. Assign homework *Questions 1–10* in the *Student Guide.* **Assessment** 1. Use *Questions 5–6* in the Homework section to assess students' skills. 2. Use DPP Task T *Comparing Fractions* as a quiz.	• crayons or markers	• 3–4 copies of *Centimeter Dot Paper* URG Page 36 per student • 1 transparency of *Centimeter Dot Paper* URG Page 36
Lesson 7 **Adding and Subtracting Fractions** URG Pages 110–123 SG Pages 177–181 DPP U–V HP Part 6 *Estimated Class Sessions* **1-2**	**Activity** Students use rectangles on dot paper to subtract fractions. Then they develop paper-and-pencil procedures for adding and subtracting fractions. **Homework** 1. Assign homework *Questions 1–8* in the *Student Guide.* 2. Assign Part 6 of the Home Practice. **Assessment** Students complete the *Fraction Follow-Up* Assessment Pages.		• 1 copy of *Fraction Follow-Up* URG Pages 117–118 per student • 3–4 copies of *Centimeter Dot Paper* URG Page 36 per student • 1 transparency of *Centimeter Dot Paper* URG Page 36
Lesson 8 **Shannon's Trip to School** URG Pages 124–128 SG Page 182 HP Part 7 *Estimated Class Sessions* **1**	OPTIONAL LESSON **Optional Activity** Students complete a set of word problems using fractions. **Homework** 1. Assign some or all of the problems for homework. 2. Assign Part 7 of the Home Practice. **Assessment** Use any of the problems for assessment.	• 1 calculator per student	

Connections

A current list of literature and software connections is available at *www.mathtrailblazers.com.* You can also find information on connections in the *Teacher Implementation Guide* Literature List and Software List sections.

Software Connections

- *Fraction Attraction* develops understanding of fractions using fraction bars, pie charts, hundreds blocks, and other materials.
- *Math Arena* is a collection of math activities that reinforces many math concepts.
- *Math Munchers Deluxe* provides practice in basic facts and finding equivalent fractions, decimals, percents, ratios, angles and identifying geometric shapes, factors, and multiples in an arcade-like game.
- *Math Mysteries: Fractions* develops problem solving with fractions.
- *Mighty Math Number Heroes* poses short answer questions about fractions, number operations, polygons, and probability.
- *National Library of Virtual Manipulatives* website (http://matti.usu.edu) allows students to work with manipulatives including geoboards, base-ten pieces, the abacus, and many others.
- *Tenth Planet: Fraction Operations* develops conceptual understanding of fraction operations, including finding common denominators.

Teaching All Math Trailblazers Students

Math Trailblazers® lessons are designed for students with a wide range of abilities. The lessons are flexible and do not require significant adaptation for diverse learning styles or academic levels. However, when needed, lessons can be tailored to allow students to engage their abilities to the greatest extent possible while building knowledge and skills.

To assist you in meeting the needs of all students in your classroom, this section contains information about some of the features in the curriculum that allow all students access to mathematics. For additional information, see the Teaching the *Math Trailblazers* Student: Meeting Individual Needs section in the *Teacher Implementation Guide.*

Differentiation Opportunities in this Unit

Games

Use games to promote or extend understanding of math concepts and to practice skills with children who need more practice.

- *Fraction Cover-All* from Lesson 3 *Using Dot Paper Rectangles*

Laboratory Experiments

Laboratory experiments enable students to solve problems using a variety of representations including pictures, tables, graphs, and symbols. Teachers can assign or adapt parts of the analysis according to the student's ability. The following lesson is a lab:

- Lesson 5 *A Day at the Races*

Journal Prompts

Journal prompts provide opportunities for students to explain and reflect on mathematical problems. They can help both students who need practice explaining their ideas and students who benefit from answering higher order questions. Students with various learning styles can express themselves using pictures, words, and sentences. Teachers can alter journal prompts to suit students' ability levels. The following lessons contain a journal prompt:

- Lesson 1 *Geoboard Fractions*
- Lesson 2 *Parts and Wholes*
- Lesson 6 *Adding Fractions with Rectangles*
- Lesson 7 *Adding and Subtracting Fractions*

DPP Challenges

DPP Challenges are items from the Daily Practice and Problems that usually take more than fifteen minutes to complete. These problems are more thought-provoking and can be used to stretch students' problem-solving skills. The following lessons have DPP Challenges in them:

- DPP Challenge D from Lesson 1 *Geoboard Fractions*
- DPP Challenge F from Lesson 2 *Parts and Wholes*
- DPP Challenge J from Lesson 4 *Using Common Denominators*
- DPP Challenges L and P from Lesson 5 *A Day at the Races*
- DPP Challenge V from Lesson 7 *Adding and Subtracting Fractions*

Extensions

Use extensions to enrich lessons. Many extensions provide opportunities to further involve or challenge students of all abilities. Take a moment to review the extensions prior to beginning this unit. Some extensions may require additional preparation and planning. The following lessons contain extensions:

- Lesson 2 *Parts and Wholes*
- Lesson 3 *Using Dot Paper Rectangles*
- Lesson 4 *Using Common Denominators*
- Lesson 5 *A Day at the Races*
- Lesson 7 *Adding and Subtracting Fractions*

Background
Investigating Fractions

This unit connects two important strands in the curriculum: the study of fractions and the use of data to solve problems. Students extend their knowledge of fraction concepts to include models for finding common denominators. Using these models, they develop procedures for comparing, adding, and subtracting fractions with unlike denominators. In the lab *A Day at the Races,* students apply fraction concepts as they collect, display, and analyze data. They also compare speeds using graphs and ratios expressed as fractions.

Modeling Fractions

This unit builds on concepts and procedures studied in Unit 3 *Fractions and Ratios* using a new part-whole model for representing fractions. Students learn to build rectangles on geoboards and draw rectangles on dot paper to represent fractions. See Figure 1.

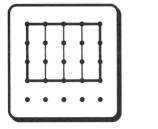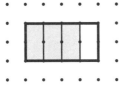

Figure 1: *A rectangle on a geoboard divided into fourths and a rectangle on dot paper modeling $\frac{3}{4}$*

Figure 2 shows two different ways to divide a 3 × 4 rectangle into fourths. In the rectangle on the left, all four of the fractional parts are congruent. In the other rectangle, there are two different shapes for the fractional parts. All the parts are fourths, however, because each part has an area of 3 square units. The area model for fractions is explored with geoboards, dot paper, and pattern blocks and these models are linked with symbols ($\frac{1}{4}$) and words (one-fourth).

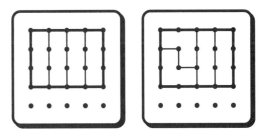

Figure 2: *Dividing a 3 × 4 rectangle into fourths*

The area model helps students develop a conceptual understanding of common denominators. For example, students consider which is larger, $\frac{3}{4}$ or $\frac{2}{3}$, by first looking for a rectangle that can be divided into both thirds and fourths on dot paper or a geoboard. The 3 × 4 rectangle on the left in Figure 3 is divided into fourths and shows $\frac{3}{4}$; the one on the right is divided into thirds and shows $\frac{2}{3}$. By counting the unit squares, each of which has an area of $\frac{1}{12}$ of the rectangle, students see that $\frac{3}{4}$ (or $\frac{9}{12}$) is larger than $\frac{2}{3}$ (or $\frac{8}{12}$). See Figure 4.

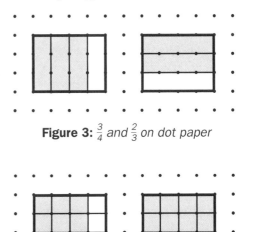

Figure 3: $\frac{3}{4}$ *and* $\frac{2}{3}$ *on dot paper*

Figure 4: $\frac{9}{12}$ *and* $\frac{8}{12}$ *on dot paper*

In the final lessons of this unit, students add and subtract fractions with unlike denominators.

Before they begin, they develop strategies for estimating sums and differences so they will know if their answers make sense. Then they model the addition and subtraction using rectangles on dot paper. Finally, they use symbols to add and subtract. These lessons emphasize the concepts involved in the procedures. Students do not need to give answers in lowest terms or change improper fractions to mixed numbers. Instead, as students solve problems, encourage them to concentrate on using meaningful procedures and make connections between the models and the symbols. In later units, students have opportunities to further develop efficient pencil-and-paper procedures for adding and subtracting fractions.

Research strongly supports using manipulatives in classrooms from the elementary to secondary level. As older elementary students develop their own learning styles, they should be free to choose from a variety of manipulatives and models. One of your jobs in this unit is to help students make connections between pattern block fractions, fractions modeled on geoboards and dot paper, and symbolic representations.

Using Data

Through the study of five fundamental variables—length, area, mass, volume, and time—students using *Math Trailblazers* make connections between math and science. Students explore these variables in kindergarten, and they investigate them in the labs in Grades 1–5. At each grade level, students use each variable with increasing sophistication. For example, in first grade, students measure volume by counting the number of identical objects that will fill a container or by counting the number of cubes needed to build an object. In second grade, students learn to measure volume by displacement, and they use this skill again in third and fourth grades in different contexts.

You can measure these basic variables with a single direct measurement. (Volume can be measured directly with a graduated cylinder.) In fifth grade, students move on to compound variables such as density and speed. Density (or mass per unit volume) is a compound variable because it involves both mass and volume. To find the density of an object, you need to measure both its mass and its volume. For more information on variables, see the TIMS Tutor: *The TIMS Laboratory Method* in the *Teacher Implementation Guide*.

In Unit 3, students began their investigations of compound variables. They learned that speed is the ratio of distance traveled to time taken. To find the walking speed of a student, they measured both distance and time and graphed the data. The data points formed a straight line through (0,0) and students used the line to help them write speed as a ratio (distance traveled/time taken). In this unit, students continue to investigate speed using both ratios and graphs. In the lab *A Day at the Races,* they measure the distance traveled and the time taken by students who are moving at different speeds by walking, running, hopping, crawling, etc. When they graph the data, they draw a line to represent each speed as shown in Figure 5. Then they use the graph to compare speeds: the steeper the line, the greater the speed. These pre-algebra skills and concepts will be used again when students investigate density in Unit 13 and the circumference of a circle in Unit 14.

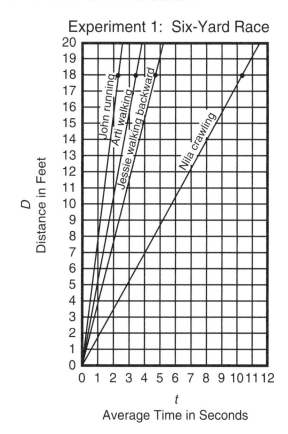

Figure 5: *Lines to represent speeds*

Resources

- Behr, M.J., and T.R. Post. "Teaching Rational Number and Decimal Concepts." In *Teaching Mathematics in Grades K–8: Research Based Methods.* Allyn and Bacon, Boston, 1992.

- Caldwell, J.H. "Communicating about Fractions with Pattern Blocks." In *Teaching Children Mathematics,* 2 (3), National Council of Teachers of Mathematics, Reston, VA, November 1995.
- Cramer, K., M. Behr, and T. Post. *Rational Number Project: Fraction Lessons for the Middle Grades—Levels 1 and 2.* Kendall/Hunt, Dubuque, IA, 1998.
- Cramer, K., and T.R. Post. "Making Connections: A Case for Proportionality." In *Arithmetic Teacher,* 40 (6), National Council of Teachers of Mathematics, Reston, VA, February 1993.
- Curcio, F.R., and N.S. Bezuk. *Understanding Rational Numbers and Proportions.* National Council of Teachers of Mathematics, Reston, VA, 1994.
- Kouba, et al. "Result of the Fourth NAEP Assessment of Mathematics: Number, Operations, and Word Problems" in *Arithmetic Teacher,* 35 (8), April 1988.
- Mack, N.K. "Learning Fractions with Understanding: Building on Informal Knowledge." In *Journal for Research in Mathematics Education,* 21 (1), National Council of Teachers of Mathematics, Reston, VA, January 1990.
- Post, T.R., et al. "Order and Equivalence of Rational Numbers: A Cognitive Analysis." In *Journal for Research in Mathematics Education,* 16 (1), National Council of Teachers of Mathematics, Reston, VA, January 1985.
- *Principles and Standards for School Mathematics.* National Council of Teachers of Mathematics, Reston, VA, 2000.
- Suydam, Marilyn. "Manipulatives, Materials, and Achievement" in *Arithmetic Teacher,* 33 (6), February 1986.
- Trafton, Paul, and Albert P. Shulte, (editors). *New Directions for Elementary School Mathematics, 1989 Yearbook.* National Council of Teachers of Mathematics, Reston, VA, 1989.

Observational Assessment Record

A1 Can students represent fractions using pattern blocks and rectangles on dot paper?

A2 Can students find equivalent fractions?

A3 Can students compare and order fractions?

A4 Can students collect, organize, graph, and analyze data?

A5 Can students draw and interpret best-fit lines?

A6 Can students use ratios to solve problems?

A7 Can students measure length in yards and feet?

A8 Can students add and subtract fractions using manipulatives, pictures, or symbols?

A9 Do students demonstrate fluency with the multiplication and division facts for the 9s?

A10 _____

Name	A1	A2	A3	A4	A5	A6	A7	A8	A9	A10	Comments
1.											
2.											
3.											
4.											
5.											
6.											
7.											
8.											
9.											
10.											
11.											
12.											
13.											

Name	A1	A2	A3	A4	A5	A6	A7	A8	A9	A10	Comments
14.											
15.											
16.											
17.											
18.											
19.											
20.											
21.											
22.											
23.											
24.											
25.											
26.											
27.											
28.											
29.											
30.											
31.											
32.											

Unit 5

Daily Practice and Problems
Investigating Fractions

A DPP Menu for Unit 5

Two Daily Practice and Problems (DPP) items are included for each class session listed in the Unit Outline. A scope and sequence chart for the DPP is in the *Teacher Implementation Guide*.

Icons in the Teacher Notes column designate the subject matter of each DPP item. The first item in each class session is always a Bit and the second is either a Task or Challenge. Each item falls into one or more of the categories listed below. A menu of the DPP items for Unit 5 follows.

N Number Sense	✖ Computation	🕐 Time	🖢 Geometry
E, F, J, L, Q, R, T, V	D–H, M, N, P	A, P	L

⁵⁄ₓ₇ Math Facts	$ Money	⚖ Measurement	▨ Data
B–E, I, K, O, S	H	J, U	

The *Daily Practice and Problems and Home Practice Guide* in the *Teacher Implementation Guide* includes information on how and when to use the DPP.

Review and Assessment of Math Facts

By the end of fourth grade, students in *Math Trailblazers* are expected to demonstrate fluency with all the multiplication and division facts. The DPP for this unit continues the systematic, strategies-based approach to reviewing the multiplication and division facts. This unit reviews the fourth group of facts, the 9s. The *Triangle Flash Cards* for these facts follow the Home Practice for this unit in the *Discovery Assignment Book*. Blackline masters of all the cards, organized by group, are in the *Grade 5 Facts Resource Guide*.

The following describes the now familiar procedure of how the facts for the 9s will be practiced and assessed in the DPP for this unit.

1. DPP item B instructs students to quiz each other on the multiplication and division facts for the 9s using the *Triangle Flash Cards*. Students sort the cards into three piles: those facts they know and can answer quickly, those they can figure out with a strategy, and those they need to learn. The DPP item also reminds students to update their *Multiplication* and *Division Facts I Know* charts, which they began in Lesson 2 of Unit 2.

2. DPP items C and E help students practice the multiplication facts for the 9s. DPP items I, K, and O use fact families to practice the related division facts.

3. DPP item S assesses students on a mixture of multiplication and division facts. Students update both their *Multiplication* and *Division Facts I Know* charts.

Note: Part 1 of the Home Practice in the *Discovery Assignment Book* reminds students to take home their flash cards to practice the facts with a family member.

For more information about the distribution and assessment of the math facts, see the TIMS Tutor: *Math Facts* in the *Teacher Implementation Guide.* Also refer to the *Grade 5 Facts Resource Guide.*

 **Daily Practice and Problems**

Students may solve the items individually, in groups, or as a class. The items may also be assigned for homework. The DPPs are also available on the Teacher Resource CD.

Student Questions	Teacher Notes

 All Aboard!

The Sydney train in Australia takes 8 minutes to travel between each station. It stays at each station for 3 minutes. There are 4 stations in between Canterbury and Parramatta. At what time will the train arrive in Parramatta if it left Canterbury at 5:22 P.M.? (*Hint:* Make a drawing.)

TIMS Bit

$5 \times 8 = 40$ minutes of travel time

$4 \times 3 = 12$ minutes at the four stations in between Parramatta and Canterbury

52 minutes after 5:22 P.M. is 6:14 P.M.

B **Multiplication and Division Facts: 9s**

With a partner, use your *Triangle Flash Cards* to quiz each other on the multiplication and division facts for the 9s. Follow the directions in the *Student Guide* for Unit 2 Lesson 2 *Facts I Know.*

As your partner quizzes you on the multiplication facts, separate the facts into three piles: those facts you know and can answer quickly, those you can figure out with a strategy, and those you need to learn. Practice any facts for the 9s in the last two piles. List these facts so you can practice them at home. Repeat the process for the division facts.

Circle all the facts you know and can answer quickly on your *Multiplication* and *Division Facts I Know* charts.

TIMS Task

The *Triangle Flash Cards: 9s* are in the *Discovery Assignment Book* following the Home Practice. Blackline masters of all the flash cards, organized by group, are in the *Grade 5 Facts Resource Guide.* Part 1 of the Home Practice reminds students to take home the list of 9s they need to study as well as their flash cards.

The *Multiplication* and *Division Facts I Know* charts were distributed in the *Unit Resource Guide* for Unit 2 Lesson 2. See that Lesson Guide or the *Grade 5 Facts Resource Guide* for more information.

Inform students when you will give the quiz on these facts. This assessment appears in DPP item S.

Student Questions	Teacher Notes

C **Order of Operations**

A. $20 \div 5 \times 9 =$ B. $18 - 3 \times 3 =$

C. $3 + 9 \times 3 =$ D. $(6 + 3) \times 8 =$

TIMS Bit

A. 36

B. 9

C. 30

D. 72

D **How Many Answers?**

Leaving the numbers in the order given, use operations $(+, -, \times, \div)$ and parentheses to get as many different answers as you can. You may use an operation more than once.

Example: 2   4   6

$2 + 4 \times 6 = 26$

$(2 + 4) \times 6 = 36$

$(2 + 4) \div 6 = 1$

A. 25   5   10

B. 30   6   2

Only whole numbers are allowed at each step. For example, $2 \div 4 + 6$ is not allowed, since $2 \div 4 = \frac{1}{2}$.

TIMS Challenge

A. Some possibilities are:
   $25 \div 5 \times 10 = 50$;
   $(25 + 5) \div 10 = 3$;
   $(25 - 5) \div 10 = 2$

B. Some possibilities are:
   $30 \div 6 + 2 = 7$;
   $30 \times 6 \div 2 = 90$;
   $(30 - 6) \times 2 = 48$;
   $30 - 6 \times 2 = 18$;
   $30 + 6 - 2 = 34$

E **Multiplying by 10s**

A. $30 \times 90 =$ B. $80 \times 90 =$

C. $900 \times 60 =$ D. $50 \times 900 =$

E. $1000 \times 90 =$ F. $900 \times 200 =$

G. $4000 \times 900 =$ H. $70 \times 900 =$

I. $9000 \times 9 =$

TIMS Bit

A. 2700   B. 7200

C. 54,000   D. 45,000

E. 90,000   F. 180,000

G. 3,600,000   H. 63,000

I. 81,000

Averaging Scores

Every week Felicia takes a spelling test on 20 spelling words. Mr. Moreno uses the mean to average test scores. Felicia wants her average number of correct words to be 17 or greater. She spelled the following number of words correctly on the first 5 tests: 15, 18, 15, 16, and 20. What must she score on her sixth test so her average on all six will be at least 17? Explain your thinking.

TIMS Challenge

She needs to get 18 or more words correct. Students can solve this problem using connecting cubes or trial and error. Also have calculators available. Students can multiply 17 by 6 to get the total number of points Felicia needs for an average of 17 points per test; $17 \times 6 = 102$. Then they can subtract her total for the first five tests to see what she needs on the sixth test. Some students may justify a score as low as 15. A score of 15 will give an average of 16.5. If rounding is allowed, this could be rounded to 17. For the mean to equal exactly 17, Felicia must spell 18 words correctly on the sixth test.

G **Subtraction Practice**

Solve the following problems in your head.

A. $1000 - 1 =$

B. $300 - 29 =$

C. $1505 - 10 =$

D. $150 - 25 =$

E. $90 - 33 =$

F. $460 - 160 =$

TIMS Bit

Discuss students' strategies. For example, to solve $300 - 29$, a student can subtract 30 first, to get 270, and then add 1 back on for an answer of 271.

A. 999
B. 271
C. 1495
D. 125
E. 57
F. 300

Making Change

How many ways can you make change for a $50 bill using only $5 bills, $10 bills, and $20 bills?

TIMS Task

12 ways

$20	$10	$5
2	1	0
2	0	2
1	3	0
1	2	2
1	1	4
1	0	6
0	5	0
0	4	2
0	3	4
0	2	6
0	1	8
0	0	10

 Fact Families for × and ÷

Solve each pair of related facts. Then name two other facts in the same fact family.

A. $9 \times 2 = ?$ and $18 \div 2 = ?$

B. $5 \times 9 = ?$ and $45 \div 9 = ?$

C. $7 \times 9 = ?$ and $63 \div 7 = ?$

D. $9 \times 8 = ?$ and $72 \div 9 = ?$

E. $10 \times 9 = ?$ and $90 \div 10 = ?$

F. $3 \times 9 = ?$ and $27 \div 3 = ?$

G. $9 \times 6 = ?$ and $54 \div 6 = ?$

H. $9 \times 4 = ?$ and $36 \div 9 = ?$

TIMS Bit

A. 18; 9; $2 \times 9 = 18$;
   $18 \div 9 = 2$

B. 45; 5; $9 \times 5 = 45$;
   $45 \div 5 = 9$

C. 63; 9; $9 \times 7 = 63$;
   $63 \div 9 = 7$

D. 72; 8; $8 \times 9 = 72$;
   $72 \div 8 = 9$

E. 90; 9; $9 \times 10 = 90$;
   $90 \div 9 = 10$

F. 27; 9; $9 \times 3 = 27$;
   $27 \div 9 = 3$

G. 54; 9; $6 \times 9 = 54$;
   $54 \div 9 = 6$

H. 36; 4; $4 \times 9 = 36$;
   $36 \div 4 = 9$

How Many Pennies?

1. Predict how many pennies it will take to cover your desktop. The pennies must lie flat. Record your prediction.

2. Check your prediction. (*Hint:* You don't need lots and lots of pennies. How many do you need to run across the length of your desk? How many do you need to run across the width?)

3. Is your prediction within 10% of the number you calculated in Question 2? How do you know?

TIMS Challenge

Answers will vary. If students did not complete Lesson 4 *How Close Is Close Enough?* in Unit 4, do not assign Question 3.

 Fact Families for × and ÷

Complete the number sentences for the related facts.

A. $9 \times 2 =$ ___

___ $\div 9 =$ ___

___ $\div 2 =$ ___

$2 \times$ ___ $=$ ___

B. $8 \times 9 =$ ___

___ $\div$ ___ $= 8$

___ $\div 8 =$ ___

___ $\times 8 =$ ___

C. $36 \div 4 =$ ___

___ $\times 4 =$ ___

$36 \div$ ___ $=$ ___

$4 \times$ ___ $=$ ___

D. $10 \times$ ___ $= 90$

$90 \div$ ___ $=$ ___

$90 \div$ ___ $=$ ___

___ $\times 10 =$ ___

TIMS Bit

A. 18; $18 \div 9 = 2$;
$18 \div 2 = 9$;
$2 \times 9 = 18$

B. 72; $72 \div 9 = 8$;
$72 \div 8 = 9$;
$9 \times 8 = 72$

C. 9; $9 \times 4 = 36$;
$36 \div 9 = 4$;
$4 \times 9 = 36$

D. 9; $90 \div 9 = 10$;
$90 \div 10 = 9$;
$9 \times 10 = 90$

Dot Paper Fractions

If a 2 cm by 3 cm rectangle is $\frac{3}{4}$, show one whole using rectangles on dot paper.

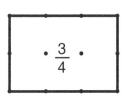

TIMS Challenge

A 2 × 4 rectangle is one whole.

 Division

Use a paper-and-pencil method to solve the following. Estimate to make sure your answers make sense.

A. $2718 \div 9 =$ B. $8672 \div 9 =$

C. $7348 \div 9 =$ D. $4977 \div 9 =$

TIMS Bit

A. 302

B. 963 R5

C. 816 R4

D. 553

N **Let's Practice**

1. Solve the following problems using paper and pencil only. Estimate to make sure your answers are reasonable.

   A. $18 \times 63 =$

   B. $565 + 739 =$

   C. $2706 - 1187 =$

   D. $37 \times 29 =$

   E. $5170 \div 5 =$

   F. $17,235 \div 9 =$

2. List the answers in order from smallest to largest.

TIMS Task

1. A. 1134
   B. 1304
   C. 1519
   D. 1073
   E. 1034
   F. 1915

2. 1034; 1073; 1134; 1304; 1519; 1915

| Student Questions | Teacher Notes |

 Fact Families for × and ÷

Complete the number sentences for the related facts.

A. $3 \times 9 = $ ___

___ $\div 3 = $ ___

___ $\div 9 = $ ___

___ $\times 3 = $ ___

B. $9 \times 7 = $ ___

___ $\div 7 = $ ___

___ $\div 9 = $ ___

$7 \times $ ___ $ = $ ___

C. $9 \times 9 = $ ___

___ $\div 9 = $ ___

D. $54 \div 6 = $ ___

___ $\times 6 = $ ___

$54 \div $ ___ $ = $ ___

___ $\times 9 = $ ___

E. $9 \times 5 = $ ___

___ $\div 9 = $ ___

___ $\div 5 = $ ___

___ $\times 9 = $ ___

TIMS Bit

A. 27; $27 \div 3 = 9$;
$27 \div 9 = 3$;
$9 \times 3 = 27$

B. 63; $63 \div 7 = 9$;
$63 \div 9 = 7$;
$7 \times 9 = 63$

C. 81; $81 \div 9 = 9$

D. 9; $9 \times 6 = 54$;
$54 \div 9 = 6$;
$6 \times 9 = 54$

E. 45; $45 \div 9 = 5$;
$45 \div 5 = 9$;
$5 \times 9 = 45$

 The Backward Race

Jackie's speed in the Backward Race was $\frac{18 \text{ feet}}{2.5 \text{ seconds}}$. If she can travel at this same rate for 1 hour, how many feet will Jackie travel? How many yards is this?

TIMS Challenge

$\frac{18 \text{ feet}}{2.5 \text{ seconds}} = \frac{36 \text{ feet}}{5 \text{ seconds}} = $

$\frac{432 \text{ feet}}{60 \text{ seconds}} = \frac{25{,}920 \text{ feet}}{3600 \text{ seconds}}$ or

$\frac{8640 \text{ yards}}{1 \text{ hour}}$

Student Questions	Teacher Notes

 Estimating Answer Size

Without solving these problems on paper, name the number of digits in the answer.

A. $112 + 658$

B. $122 + 967$

C. $1221 - 345$

D. $3042 - 1132$

E. 5×520

TIMS Bit

Students should be ready to defend their answers when given.

A. 3 digits

B. 4 digits

C. 3 digits

D. 4 digits

E. 4 digits

R **Estimating Sums**

Estimate each sum using the benchmarks 0, $\frac{1}{2}$, and 1 to help you. You may use the Number Lines for Fractohoppers chart in the *Student Guide* in Unit 3 Lesson 4.

A. $\frac{4}{5} + \frac{7}{8} =$

B. $\frac{3}{9} - \frac{3}{8} =$

C. $\frac{1}{12} + \frac{3}{7} + \frac{5}{8} =$

D. $\frac{7}{11} - \frac{2}{9} =$

E. $\frac{4}{5} - \frac{3}{8} =$

F. $\frac{1}{12} + \frac{5}{10} =$

TIMS Task

A. About 2 B. About 0

C. About 1 D. About $\frac{1}{2}$

E. About $\frac{1}{2}$ F. About $\frac{1}{2}$

S **Quiz: 9s**

A. $9 \times 5 =$

B. $18 \div 2 =$

C. $27 \div 9 =$

D. $9 \times 10 =$

E. $8 \times 9 =$

F. $4 \times 9 =$

G. $81 \div 9 =$

H. $7 \times 9 =$

I. $54 \div 6 =$

TIMS Bit

We recommend 2 minutes for this quiz. Allow students to change pens after the time is up and complete the remaining problems in a different color. Have them update their *Multiplication Facts I Know* and *Division Facts I Know* charts.

Student Questions	Teacher Notes

 Comparing Fractions

Write a number sentence to compare the following fractions. Use $<$, $>$, or $=$ in your sentence. Explain your thinking for Questions A and B. Be prepared to share your strategies for the others.

A. $\frac{1}{10}, \frac{7}{8}$ B. $\frac{4}{8}, \frac{5}{10}$ C. $\frac{4}{5}, \frac{1}{2}$

D. $\frac{2}{3}, \frac{7}{12}$ E. $\frac{3}{10}, \frac{3}{8}$ F. $\frac{11}{12}, \frac{5}{12}$

TIMS Task

A. $\frac{1}{10} < \frac{7}{8}$

Possible response: Since $\frac{1}{10}$ is close to 0 and $\frac{7}{8}$ is close to 1, $\frac{1}{10}$ is smaller than $\frac{7}{8}$.

B. $\frac{4}{8} = \frac{5}{10}$

Possible response: Since 4 is half of 8 and 5 is half of 10, then both fractions are equal to $\frac{1}{2}$.

C. $\frac{4}{5} > \frac{1}{2}$ D. $\frac{2}{3} > \frac{7}{12}$

E. $\frac{3}{10} < \frac{3}{8}$ F. $\frac{11}{12} > \frac{5}{12}$

 Choosing Units of Measure

The following are some units of measure for length: meters, centimeters, feet, inches, yards, kilometers, and miles.

Which unit of measure does it make sense to use when you measure:

1. the length of a book?

2. the distance from your classroom door to your teacher's desk?

3. the distance from your home to school?

4. a person's height?

TIMS Bit

Answers will vary.

1. centimeters, inches

2. feet, meters, centimeters, inches, yards

3. For some students who live across the street or around the corner, they might say feet or yards. Others who take the bus to school might say miles or kilometers.

4. feet and inches, centimeters

V **Scale Models**

Frank and John both are making models of a building in their town. In John's building, 2 inches of the model represent 5 feet of the real building. In Frank's building, 5 inches represent 15 feet. Whose model will be larger? Explain why you think so.

TIMS Challenge

Solution strategies will vary. One possible strategy:

John: $\frac{2 \text{ inches}}{5 \text{ feet}} = \frac{6 \text{ inches}}{15 \text{ feet}}$

Frank: $\frac{5 \text{ inches}}{15 \text{ feet}}$

$\frac{6 \text{ inches}}{15 \text{ feet}} > \frac{5 \text{ inches}}{15 \text{ feet}}$

John's building will be larger.

Geoboard Fractions

Lesson Overview

Estimated Class Sessions **2-3**

Students explore fractions and mixed numbers using geoboards and rectangles on dot paper. They review the terms denominator and numerator. Given a rectangle representing one whole, students show different ways to represent fractions of the whole and fractions greater than one.

Key Content

- Finding a fraction for a given quantity when a unit whole is given.
- Representing fractions and mixed numbers using geoboards, pictures, and symbols.

Key Vocabulary

- denominator
- fraction
- numerator

Math Facts

Complete DPP items B–D and begin reviewing the multiplication and division facts for the 9s.

Homework

1. Assign the Homework section in the *Student Guide*.
2. Assign Part 1 of the Home Practice.

Assessment

Use *Questions 5–6* from the Homework section to assess students' understanding of denominators and numerators.

Curriculum Sequence

Before This Unit

Students used pattern blocks and number lines to model fractions in Unit 3. They named fractions when given the whole, ordered fractions, found equivalent fractions, and wrote fractions greater than one as mixed numbers and improper fractions.

After This Unit

Students will continue the study of fractions and their connections to decimals and percents in Units 7, 8, 9, and 11. In Unit 12 students practice pencil-and-paper procedures for adding, subtracting, and multiplying fractions.

Materials List

Supplies and Copies

Student	Teacher
Supplies for Each Student Pair • geoboard • rubber bands	**Supplies** • overhead geoboard • rubber bands
Copies • 4–5 copies of *Centimeter Dot Paper* per student (*Unit Resource Guide* Page 36)	**Copies/Transparencies** • 1 transparency of *Centimeter Dot Paper* (*Unit Resource Guide* Page 36)

All blackline masters including assessment, transparency, and DPP masters are also on the Teacher Resource CD.

Student Books
Geoboard Fractions (*Student Guide* Pages 144–151)
Triangle Flash Cards: 9s (*Discovery Assignment Book* Pages 75–76)

Daily Practice and Problems and Home Practice
DPP items A–D (*Unit Resource Guide* Pages 17–18)
Home Practice Part 1 (*Discovery Assignment Book* Page 71)

Note: Classrooms whose pacing differs significantly from the suggested pacing of the units should use the Math Facts Calendar in Section 4 of the *Facts Resource Guide* to ensure students receive the complete math facts program.

Daily Practice and Problems

Suggestions for using the DPPs are on pages 33–34.

A. Bit: All Aboard! (URG p. 17)

The Sydney train in Australia takes 8 minutes to travel between each station. It stays at each station for 3 minutes. There are 4 stations in between Canterbury and Parramatta. At what time will the train arrive in Parramatta if it left Canterbury at 5:22 P.M.? (*Hint:* Make a drawing.)

B. Task: Multiplication and Division Facts: 9s (URG p. 17)

With a partner, use your *Triangle Flash Cards* to quiz each other on the multiplication and division facts for the 9s. Follow the directions in the *Student Guide* for Unit 2 Lesson 2 *Facts I Know.*

As your partner quizzes you on the multiplication facts, separate the facts into three piles: those facts you know and can answer quickly, those you can figure out with a strategy, and those you need to learn. Practice any facts for the 9s in the last two piles. List these facts so you can practice them at home. Repeat the process for the division facts.

Circle all the facts you know and can answer quickly on your *Multiplication* and *Division Facts I Know* charts.

C. Bit: Order of Operations (URG p. 18)

A. $20 \div 5 \times 9 =$ B. $18 - 3 \times 3 =$

C. $3 + 9 \times 3 =$ D. $(6 + 3) \times 8 =$

D. Challenge: How Many Answers?
(URG p. 18)

Leaving the numbers in the order given, use operations $(+, -, \times, \div)$ and parentheses to get as many different answers as you can. You may use an operation more than once.

$$\text{Example: } 2 \quad 4 \quad 6$$
$$2 + 4 \times 6 = 26$$
$$(2 + 4) \times 6 = 36$$
$$(2 + 4) \div 6 = 1$$

A. 25   5   10

B. 30   6   2

Only whole numbers are allowed at each step. For example, $2 \div 4 + 6$ is not allowed, since $2 \div 4 = \frac{1}{2}$.

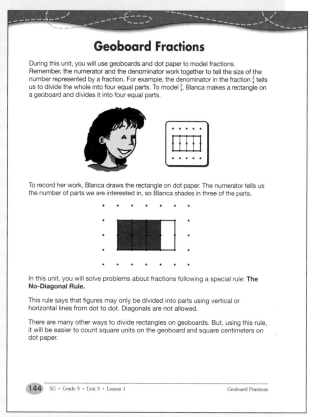

Geoboard Fractions

During this unit, you will use geoboards and dot paper to model fractions. Remember, the numerator and denominator work together to tell the size of the number represented by a fraction. For example, the denominator in the fraction $\frac{3}{4}$ tells us to divide the whole into four equal parts. To model $\frac{3}{4}$, Blanca makes a rectangle on a geoboard and divides it into four equal parts.

To record her work, Blanca draws the rectangle on dot paper. The numerator tells us the number of parts we are interested in, so Blanca shades in three of the parts.

In this unit, you will solve problems about fractions following a special rule: **The No-Diagonal Rule.**

This rule says that figures may only be divided into parts using vertical or horizontal lines from dot to dot. Diagonals are not allowed.

There are many other ways to divide rectangles on geoboards. But, using this rule, it will be easier to count square units on the geoboard and square centimeters on dot paper.

144   SG • Grade 5 • Unit 5 • Lesson 1   Geoboard Fractions

Student Guide - page 144

Content Note

The No-Diagonal Rule. This rule ensures that the smallest squares on the geoboard and centimeter squares on dot paper will remain intact. Using the rule, students can easily count square units. For example, when a 3 × 4 rectangle is divided in fourths using the no-diagonal rule, each fourth is made up of 3 small squares. Since each square is one square unit on the geoboard (or one square centimeter on dot paper), students can easily count squares to find the area and convince themselves that they have divided the rectangle into fourths. Figure 7 shows two ways to divide a 3 × 4 rectangle into fourths using the no-diagonal rule. Note that each fractional part has the same area (3 sq units) but not the same shape.

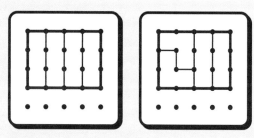

Figure 7: *Dividing a 3 × 4 rectangle into fourths using the no-diagonal rule*

Review the terms numerator and denominator using the *Geoboard Fractions* Activity Pages in the *Student Guide.* It is important that students recognize that the numerator and denominator work together to represent a fraction. Use the overhead geoboard or a transparency of *Centimeter Dot Paper* to build the fraction $\frac{3}{4}$ as shown in the *Student Guide.*

Part 1   **No-Diagonal Rule**

This lesson introduces a new model for studying fractions. Students build rectangles on geoboards or draw rectangles on dot paper to represent one whole and fractions of the whole. Just as different pattern blocks were used to represent one whole, different size rectangles are used to represent one whole. This model is used to develop procedures that use common denominators: comparing, adding, and subtracting fractions.

To facilitate the development of these procedures, students follow the no-diagonal rule: They may divide figures into parts using vertical or horizontal lines from dot to dot. Diagonals are not allowed. In Figure 6, Rectangles A and B are divided into halves using the no-diagonal rule. Rectangles C and D do not follow the rule.

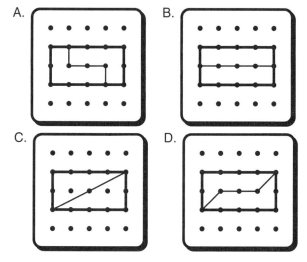

Figure 6: *Making halves using the no-diagonal rule, solutions A and B are allowed, but solutions C and D are not allowed.*

Pass out a geoboard and some rubber bands to each student pair. Explain they will use rectangles on geoboards and dot paper to solve problems about fractions. Introduce the no-diagonal rule using the sample problem.

Work through the sample problem in the *Student Guide* with students. There are three different solutions to this problem. Two solutions are shown in Figure 6 and in the *Student Guide.* Allow students to explore and to share their solutions. Ask students to evaluate solutions using the no-diagonal rule. Record the valid solutions using your transparency of *Centimeter Dot Paper.*

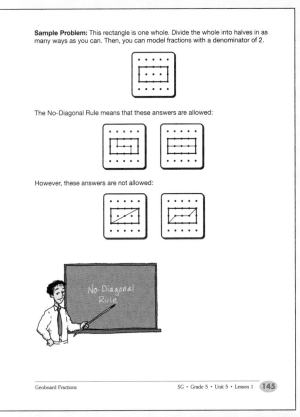

Student Guide - page 145

Part 2 Denominators: Dividing the Whole into Equal Parts

Once students understand how to use the geoboard to build fractions using rectangles and the no-diagonal rule, they can begin working in pairs on *Question 1* in the *Student Guide.* Students should record their solutions on dot paper. When students complete *Question 1,* ask:

• *How is the area of the rectangle related to the denominators that can be used to divide the rectangle?* (Students may say that the denominator is a factor of the total area or that the denominator divides the total area evenly. Since 8 can be divided evenly by 2, 4, and 8, a rectangle with an area of 8 square units can be divided into halves, fourths, and eighths, but not thirds, fifths, or sixths.)

Part 3 Numerators: Using Equal Parts of the Whole

Students continue to work in pairs. One possible method for student pairs to work together on *Questions 2–3* on dot paper is outlined at the beginning of this section in the *Student Guide.* Work through *Question 2* together to ensure student understanding. After students complete *Question 3,* provide time to share and discuss student responses.

Questions 4–6 explore a 3 × 4 rectangle. In *Questions 4–5* students find all the denominators that can be shown dividing the whole. (See Figure 8.) *Question 6* provides practice modeling fractions using a 3 × 4 rectangle. They can model $\frac{1}{2}, \frac{1}{3}, \frac{3}{4}, \frac{6}{6}$, and $\frac{5}{12}$ *(Questions 6A, 6B, 6C, 6E, 6F),* but not $\frac{5}{8}$ *(Question 6D).* Ask:

• *How is the area of the rectangle related to the denominators that can be used to divide the rectangle?* (All the denominators are factors of 12, the area of the rectangle. Since 12 can be divided by 2, 3, 4, 6, and 12, the rectangle can show halves, thirds, fourths, sixths, and twelfths.)

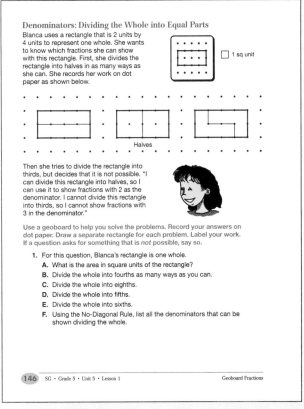

Student Guide - page 146 *(Answers on p. 37)*

Content Note

3 × 4 Rectangles. Using a 3 × 4 rectangle as one whole is analogous to using a yellow hexagon from the pattern blocks as one whole since they can be divided into halves, thirds, fourths, sixths, and twelfths.

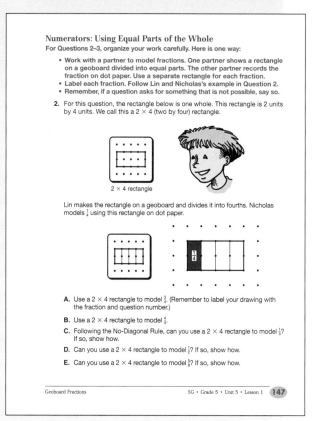

Student Guide - page 147 *(Answers on p. 37)*

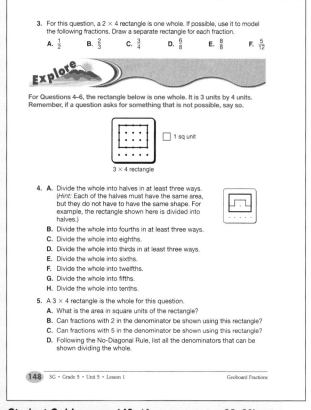

Student Guide - page 148 *(Answers on pp. 38–39)*

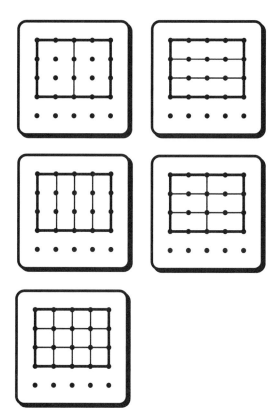

Figure 8: *Using the no-diagonal rule, a 3 × 4 rectangle can be divided into halves, thirds, fourths, sixths, and twelfths, but not fifths, eighths, or tenths.*

Questions 7–10 provide more practice modeling fractions with rectangles on dot paper. Students can work in pairs to complete them with one student

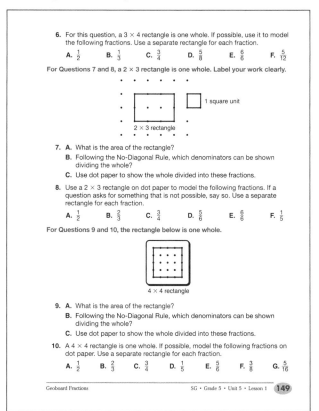

Student Guide - page 149 *(Answers on pp. 39–40)*

showing the solutions on a geoboard and the other recording them on dot paper. Or assign these problems as homework with students recording their answers on dot paper.

Part 4

Fractions Greater Than One

Questions 11–12 in the *Student Guide* ask students to model improper fractions and mixed numbers using rectangles on dot paper. Students follow the example in the *Student Guide.* See Figure 9. Note that each fraction or mixed number can be modeled in more than one way. In Lesson 6, students will use rectangles on dot paper to model addition of fractions. When they add two fractions, the sums will often be greater than one and students will need to be able to identify the sums represented on dot paper.

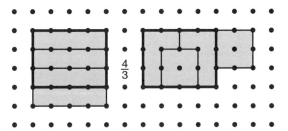

Figure 9: *Two ways to model $\frac{4}{3}$ using rectangles on dot paper. A 3 cm $\times$ 4 cm rectangle is one whole.*

TIMS Tip

Encourage students to trace around the whole rectangle with dark lines or a different color.

Math Facts

DPP item B reminds students to review the multiplication and division facts for the 9s. Items C and D review order of operations using math facts.

Homework and Practice

- Assign *Questions 7–10* in the Explore section of the *Student Guide.* Students will need dot paper to record their answers.

- Assign the Homework section in the *Student Guide.* Students will need dot paper to record their answers.

Journal Prompt

What is a fraction? How do the numerator and denominator work together to tell you the size of the number represented by the fraction?

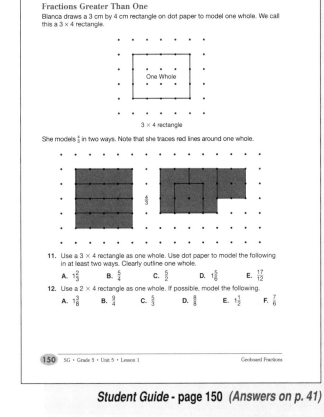

Student Guide - page 150 *(Answers on p. 41)*

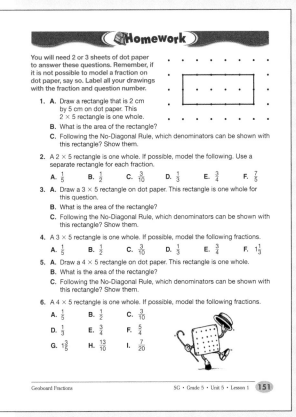

Student Guide - page 151 *(Answers on pp. 42–43)*

Unit 5 **Home Practice**

PART 1 *Triangle Flash Cards: 9s*

Study for the quiz on the multiplication and division facts for the nines. Take home your *Triangle Flash Cards: 9s* and your list of facts you need to study.

Ask a family member to choose one flash card at a time. To quiz you on a multiplication fact, he or she should cover the corner containing the highest number. Multiply the two uncovered numbers.

To quiz you on a division fact, your family member can cover one of the smaller numbers. One of the smaller numbers is circled. The other has a square around it. Use the two uncovered numbers to solve a division fact.

Ask your family member to mix up the multiplication and division facts. He or she should sometimes cover the highest number, sometimes cover the circled number, and sometimes cover the number in the square.

Your teacher will tell you when the quiz on the 9s will be given.

PART 2 **Order of Operations**

Solve the following problems using the order of operations.

A. $33 - 8 \times 3 =$ B. $35 \div 7 - 3 =$ C. $150 + 9 \times 6 =$

D. $45 \div 9 \times 4 =$ E. $100 + 200 \div 10 =$ F. $(6 + 3) \times 100 =$

G. $200 - (2 \times 70) =$ H. $60 \times 60 \div 40 =$ I. $(80 + 80) \div 40 =$

INVESTIGATING FRACTIONS   DAB • Grade 5 • Unit 5   **71**

Discovery Assignment Book - page 71

- DPP item A provides practice with elapsed time.
- Assign Part 1 of the Home Practice, which reviews math facts.

Answers for Part 1 of the Home Practice are in the Answer Key at the end of this lesson and at the end of this unit.

Assessment

Use *Questions 5–6* from the Homework section to assess students' understanding of denominators and numerators.

At a Glance

Math Facts and Daily Practice and Problems

Complete DPP items A–D and begin reviewing the multiplication and division facts for the 9s. DPP item A reviews elapsed time while items B–D review math facts.

Part 1. No-Diagonal Rule

1. Review the terms denominator and numerator.
2. Use the first page of the *Geoboard Fractions* Activity Pages in the *Student Guide* to introduce the no-diagonal rule.
3. Work through the sample problem in the *Student Guide*.

Part 2. Denominators: Dividing the Whole into Equal Parts

1. Students work in pairs on *Question 1.*
2. Discuss how the area of the rectangle chosen for one whole determines the denominators you can show dividing the whole.

Part 3. Numerators: Using Equal Parts of the Whole

1. Using *Questions 2–3,* students model fractions following the no-diagonal rule.
2. Students explore 3 × 4 rectangles. *(Questions 4–6)*
3. Students practice modeling fractions in *Questions 7–10.* You can assign these questions for homework.

Part 4. Fractions Greater Than One

Students model mixed numbers and improper fractions using rectangles on dot paper. *(Questions 11–12)*

Homework

1. Assign the Homework section in the *Student Guide*.
2. Assign Part 1 of the Home Practice.

Assessment

Use *Questions 5–6* from the Homework section to assess students' understanding of denominators and numerators.

Answer Key is on pages 37–43.

Notes:

Centimeter Dot Paper

Student Guide (p. 146)

I. A. 8 square units

B. Some possible ways are shown:

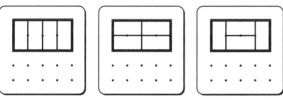

C.

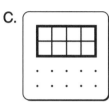

D. not possible

E. not possible

F. 2, 4, 8

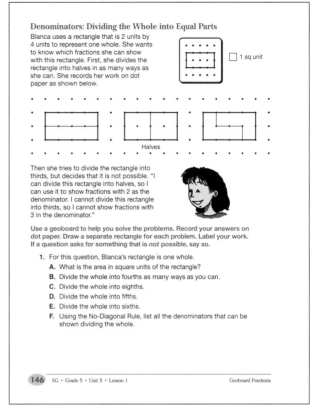

Student Guide - page 146

Student Guide (p. 147)

2. Answers will vary. The area of the fractional parts must be the same. One possible solution for each question is shown.

A.

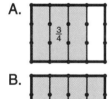

B.

C. No

D. Yes. Answers may vary.

E. Yes

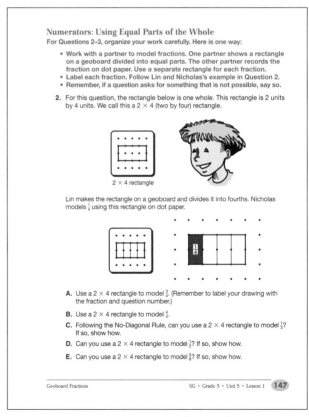

Student Guide - page 147

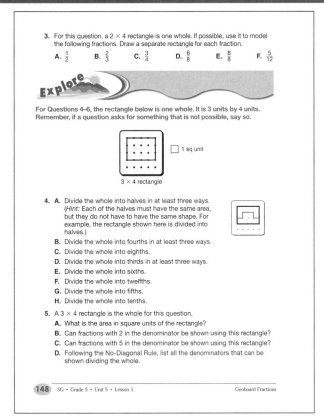

Student Guide - page 148

Student Guide (p. 148)

3. Answers will vary. The area of the fractional parts must be the same. One possible solution for each question is shown.

A.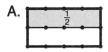

B. not possible

C.

D.

E.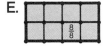

F. not possible

4. A. Some possible ways are shown:

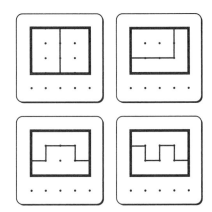

B. Some possible ways are shown:

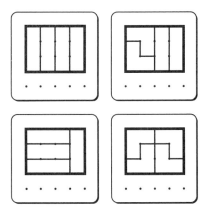

C. not possible

D. Some possible ways are shown:

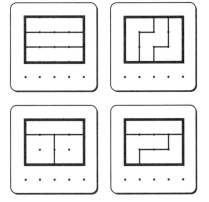

E. Some possible ways are shown:

  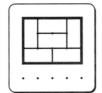

F.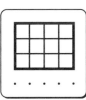
　　　　　　　G. not possible
　　　　　　　H. not possible

5. A. 12 square units*　　**B.** yes
　　C. no　　　　　　　　**D.** 2, 3, 4, 6, 12*

Student Guide (p. 149)

6. Answers will vary. The area of the fractional parts must be the same. One possible solution for each question is shown.

A.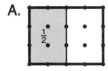

B.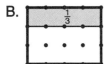

C.

D. not possible

E.

F.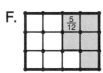

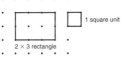

6. For this question, a 3 × 4 rectangle is one whole. If possible, use it to model the following fractions. Use a separate rectangle for each fraction.

　　A. $\frac{1}{2}$　　**B.** $\frac{1}{3}$　　**C.** $\frac{3}{4}$　　**D.** $\frac{5}{8}$　　**E.** $\frac{6}{6}$　　**F.** $\frac{5}{12}$

For Questions 7 and 8, a 2 × 3 rectangle is one whole. Label your work clearly.

1 square unit

2 × 3 rectangle

7. A. What is the area of the rectangle?
　　B. Following the No-Diagonal Rule, which denominators can be shown dividing the whole?
　　C. Use dot paper to show the whole divided into these fractions.

8. Use a 2 × 3 rectangle on dot paper to model the following fractions. If a question asks for something that is not possible, say so. Use a separate rectangle for each fraction.
　　A. $\frac{1}{2}$　　**B.** $\frac{2}{3}$　　**C.** $\frac{3}{4}$　　**D.** $\frac{5}{6}$　　**E.** $\frac{6}{6}$　　**F.** $\frac{1}{5}$

For Questions 9 and 10, the rectangle below is one whole.

4 × 4 rectangle

9. A. What is the area of the rectangle?
　　B. Following the No-Diagonal Rule, which denominators can be shown dividing the whole?
　　C. Use dot paper to show the whole divided into these fractions.

10. A 4 × 4 rectangle is one whole. If possible, model the following fractions on dot paper. Use a separate rectangle for each fraction.
　　A. $\frac{1}{2}$　　**B.** $\frac{2}{3}$　　**C.** $\frac{3}{4}$　　**D.** $\frac{1}{5}$　　**E.** $\frac{5}{6}$　　**F.** $\frac{3}{8}$　　**G.** $\frac{5}{16}$

Geoboard Fractions　　　　　　　　　　　SG • Grade 5 • Unit 5 • Lesson 1　**149**

Student Guide - page 149

*Answers and/or discussion are included in the Lesson Guide.

7. A. 6 square units

B. 2, 3, 6

C. Answers will vary. The area of the fractional parts must be the same. One possible solution for each question is shown.

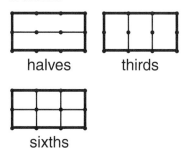

halves   thirds

sixths

8. Answers will vary. The area of the fractional parts must be the same. One possible solution for each question is shown.

A.
$\frac{1}{2}$

B.
$\frac{2}{3}$

C. not possible

D.
$\frac{5}{6}$

E.
$\frac{6}{6}$

F. not possible

9. A. 16 square units

B. 2, 4, 8, 16

C. One possible division is shown for each denominator listed in *Question 9B.*

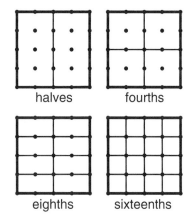

halves   fourths

eighths   sixteenths

10. Answers will vary. The area of the fractional parts must be the same. One possible solution for each question is shown.

A.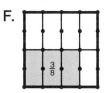
$\frac{1}{2}$

B. not possible

C.
$\frac{3}{4}$

D. not possible

E. not possible

F.
$\frac{3}{8}$

G.
$\frac{5}{16}$

Student Guide (p. 150)

11. Answers will vary. The area of the fractional parts must be the same. One possible solution for each question is shown.

A.
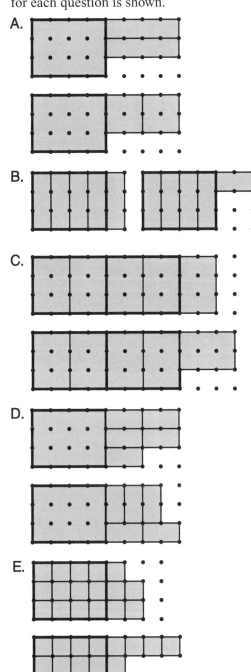

B.

C.

D.

E.

12. Answers will vary. The area of the fractional parts must be the same. One possible solution for each question is shown.

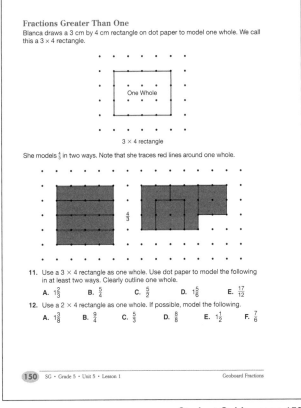

Fractions Greater Than One

Blanca draws a 3 cm by 4 cm rectangle on dot paper to model one whole. We call this a 3 × 4 rectangle.

One Whole

3 × 4 rectangle

She models $\frac{4}{3}$ in two ways. Note that she traces red lines around one whole.

$\frac{4}{3}$

11. Use a 3 × 4 rectangle as one whole. Use dot paper to model the following in at least two ways. Clearly outline one whole.
   A. $1\frac{2}{3}$ B. $\frac{5}{4}$ C. $\frac{5}{2}$ D. $1\frac{5}{6}$ E. $\frac{17}{12}$

12. Use a 2 × 4 rectangle as one whole. If possible, model the following.
   A. $1\frac{3}{8}$ B. $\frac{9}{4}$ C. $\frac{5}{3}$ D. $\frac{8}{8}$ E. $1\frac{1}{2}$ F. $\frac{7}{6}$

Geoboard Fractions

Student Guide - page 150

A.

B.
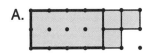

C. not possible

D.

E.
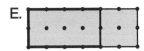

F. not possible

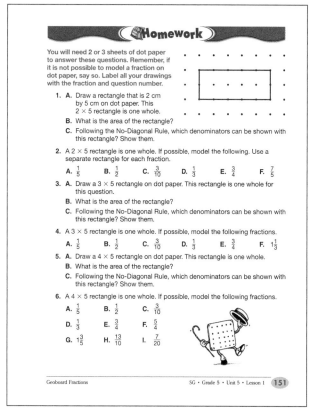

Student Guide - page 151

Student Guide (p. 151)

Homework

1. **A.**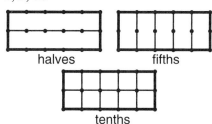

B. 10 square units

C. 2, 5, 10

halves   fifths

tenths

2. Answers will vary. The area of the fractional parts must be the same. The shaded shapes may vary.

A. $\frac{1}{5}$

B. $\frac{1}{2}$

C. $\frac{3}{10}$

D. not possible

E. not possible

F.

3. **A.**

B. 15 square units

C. 3, 5, 15

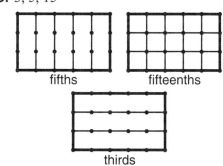

fifths   fifteenths

thirds

4. Answers will vary. The area of the fractional parts must be the same. The shaded shapes may vary.

A.

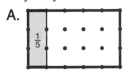

B. not possible

C. not possible

D.

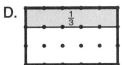

E. not possible

F.

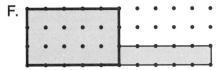

5. A.

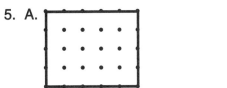

B. 20 square units

C. 2, 4, 5, 10, 20; Answers will vary.

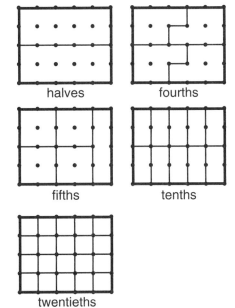

halves   fourths

fifths   tenths

twentieths

6. Answers will vary. The area of the fractional parts must be the same. The shaded shapes may vary.

A.

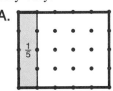

B.

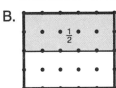

C.

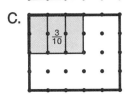

D. not possible

E.

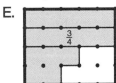

F.

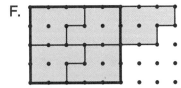

G.

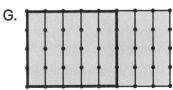

H.

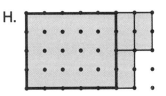

I.

Lesson 2

Parts and Wholes

Lesson Overview

Students compare fractions modeled with pattern blocks to fractions modeled with rectangles on dot paper. Then, given a fraction, they show one whole and other fractional parts of the whole.

Key Content

- Representing fractions with pattern blocks, geoboards, and pictures.
- Identifying the unit whole when a fractional part is given.

Math Facts

Assign DPP item E, which reviews math facts with multiples of ten.

Homework

1. Assign the Homework section in the *Student Guide.*
2. Assign Part 2 of the Home Practice.

Assessment

1. Use **Question 3** in the Homework section to assess students' abilities to model fractions using rectangles on dot paper.
2. Give a short quiz to assess students' abilities to represent fractions using rectangles on dot paper as you model various fractions using overhead pattern blocks.
3. Observe students as they are working in class. Record your observations on the *Observational Assessment Record* and students' *Individual Assessment Record Sheets.*

Materials List

Supplies and Copies

Student	Teacher
Supplies for Each Student Pair • 1 set of pattern blocks (2–3 yellow hexagons, 6 red trapezoids, 10 green triangles, 10 blue rhombuses, 6 brown trapezoids, 12 purple triangles)	**Supplies** • overhead pattern blocks
Copies • 3–4 copies of *Centimeter Dot Paper* per student (*Unit Resource Guide* Page 36)	**Copies/Transparencies** • 1 transparency of *Centimeter Dot Paper* (*Unit Resource Guide* Page 36) • 1 copy of *Observational Assessment Record* to be used throughout this unit (*Unit Resource Guide* Pages 13–14)

All blackline masters including assessment, transparency, and DPP masters are also on the Teacher Resource CD.

Student Books
Parts and Wholes (*Student Guide* Pages 152–156)

Daily Practice and Problems and Home Practice
DPP items E–F (*Unit Resource Guide* Pages 18–19)
Home Practice Part 2 (*Discovery Assignment Book* Page 71)

Note: Classrooms whose pacing differs significantly from the suggested pacing of the units should use the Math Facts Calendar in Section 4 of the *Facts Resource Guide* to ensure students receive the complete math facts program.

Assessment Tools
Observational Assessment Record (*Unit Resource Guide* Pages 13–14)
Individual Assessment Record Sheet (*Teacher Implementation Guide,* Assessment section)

Daily Practice and Problems

Suggestions for using the DPPs are on pages 49–50.

E. Bit: Multiplying by 10s

(URG p. 18)

A. $30 \times 90 =$ B. $80 \times 90 =$

C. $900 \times 60 =$ D. $50 \times 900 =$

E. $1000 \times 90 =$ F. $900 \times 200 =$

G. $4000 \times 900 =$ H. $70 \times 900 =$

I. $9000 \times 9 =$

F. Challenge: Averaging Scores

(URG p. 19)

Every week Felicia takes a spelling test on 20 spelling words. Mr. Moreno uses the mean to average test scores. Felicia wants her average number of correct words to be 17 or greater. She spelled the following number of words correctly on the first 5 tests: 15, 18, 15, 16, and 20. What must she score on her sixth test so her average on all six will be at least 17? Explain your thinking.

Part 1 Modeling Fractions with Pattern Blocks and Rectangles on Dot Paper

Students compare their fraction work with pattern blocks in Unit 3 with their work on the geoboards in Lesson 1 of this unit. Using overhead pattern blocks, tell students that for these problems, the yellow hexagon is one whole. Using a transparency of *Centimeter Dot Paper,* tell students that when you are using dot paper, a 3 cm × 4 cm rectangle is one whole.

Distribute *Centimeter Dot Paper* to students. Model a fraction using pattern blocks on the overhead. Ask students to model the same fraction using a 3 × 4 rectangle on dot paper. For example, if you show students a red trapezoid ($\frac{1}{2}$ of a hexagon), students should show you a 3 × 4 rectangle with 6 sq cm shaded. Two possible figures showing $\frac{1}{2}$ of a 3 × 4 rectangle are shown in Figure 10. Other figures can represent $\frac{1}{2}$ as well, as long as they have an area of 6 sq cm and follow the no-diagonal rule. (The no-diagonal rule was defined in the *Student Guide* in Lesson 1.)

Model these fractions with pattern blocks:

3 brown trapezoids ($\frac{3}{4}$),

2 blue rhombuses ($\frac{2}{3}$),

5 green triangles ($\frac{5}{6}$),

7 purple triangles ($\frac{7}{12}$),

and 3 red trapezoids ($\frac{3}{12}$).

Ask student volunteers to model fractions for the rest of the class. Model these fractions using rectangles on an overhead geoboard or a transparency of *Centimeter Dot Paper* and have students model the same fraction with pattern blocks:

$$\frac{1}{2} \quad \frac{4}{3} \quad \frac{1}{4} \quad \frac{1}{6} \quad \frac{5}{12}$$

Questions 1–3 on the *Parts and Wholes* Activity Pages in the *Student Guide* allow students to work in pairs modeling fractions using pattern blocks and rectangles on dot paper.

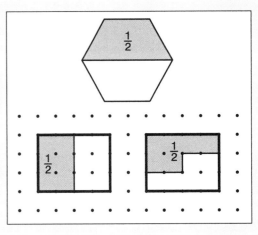

Figure 10: *Modeling $\frac{1}{2}$ using pattern blocks and dot paper*

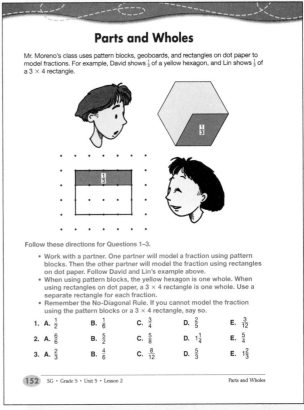

Parts and Wholes

Mr. Moreno's class uses pattern blocks, geoboards, and rectangles on dot paper to model fractions. For example, David shows $\frac{1}{3}$ of a yellow hexagon, and Lin shows $\frac{1}{3}$ of a 3 × 4 rectangle.

Follow these directions for Questions 1–3.

* Work with a partner. One partner will model a fraction using pattern blocks. Then the other partner will model the fraction using rectangles on dot paper. Follow David and Lin's example above.
* When using pattern blocks, the yellow hexagon is one whole. When using rectangles on dot paper, a 3 × 4 rectangle is one whole. Use a separate rectangle for each fraction.
* Remember the No-Diagonal Rule. If you cannot model the fraction using the pattern blocks or a 3 × 4 rectangle, say so.

1. A. $\frac{1}{2}$ B. $\frac{1}{6}$ C. $\frac{3}{4}$ D. $\frac{2}{5}$ E. $\frac{3}{12}$

2. A. $\frac{6}{6}$ B. $\frac{5}{2}$ C. $\frac{5}{8}$ D. $1\frac{1}{4}$ E. $\frac{5}{4}$

3. A. $\frac{2}{3}$ B. $\frac{4}{6}$ C. $\frac{8}{12}$ D. $\frac{5}{3}$ E. $1\frac{2}{3}$

152   SG · Grade 5 · Unit 5 · Lesson 2   Parts and Wholes

Student Guide - page 152 (Answers on p. 52)

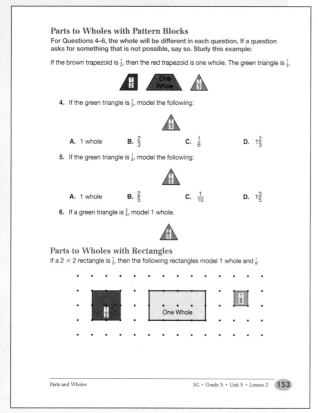

Student Guide - page 153 (Answers on p. 53)

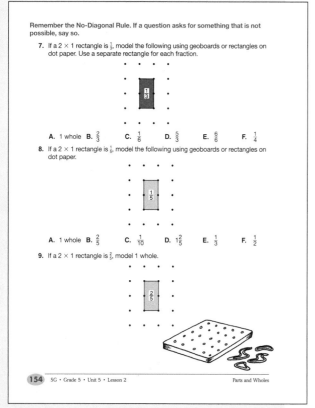

Student Guide - page 154 (Answers on p. 53)

Part 2

Parts to Wholes with Pattern Blocks

Questions 4–6 in the *Student Guide* name a fraction represented by a pattern block and ask students to model the whole. Then they model other fractional parts of the whole. For example, *Question 5* says that the green triangle is $\frac{1}{5}$. Students must then model 1 whole, $\frac{2}{5}$, $\frac{1}{10}$, and $1\frac{3}{5}$ as shown in Figure 11.

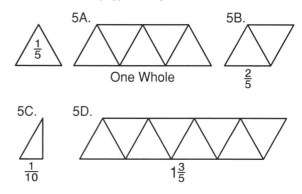

Figure 11: *Solutions to Question 5 in the Student Guide*

Part 3 **Parts to Wholes with Rectangles**

Questions 7–9 pose similar problems using rectangles. For example, in *Question 8*, a 2 × 1 rectangle is defined as $\frac{1}{5}$. Students must model six fractions. Possible solutions are shown in Figure 12. Other figures are possible. For example, to model $\frac{1}{2}$ *(Question 8F)*, other figures with an area of 5 sq cm that follow the no-diagonal rule are also allowed. However, no figure is possible to model $\frac{1}{3}$ when one whole is a 2 × 5 rectangle *(Question 8E)*. If you apply the no-diagonal rule, you cannot show fractions with denominators of 3 using a rectangle with an area of 10 sq cm since 10 cannot be divided evenly by 3.

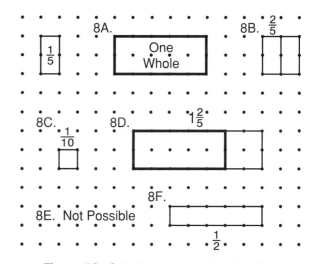

Figure 12: *Solutions to Question 8 in the Student Guide*

Questions 6 and 9 can be challenging for students. In *Question 6* the green triangle is $\frac{2}{5}$. Students can reason that if the green triangle is $\frac{2}{5}$, half the green triangle or a purple triangle is $\frac{1}{5}$. Then, 5 purple triangles are one whole as shown in Figure 13.

One Whole

Figure 13: *If the green triangle is $\frac{2}{5}$, 5 purple triangles make one whole.*

In *Question 9,* a 2 unit by 1 unit rectangle is $\frac{2}{5}$. Using similar reasoning, a figure with an area of 5 square units is one whole as shown in Figure 14.

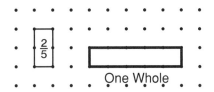
One Whole

Figure 14: *If a 2 × 1 rectangle is $\frac{2}{5}$, a 1 × 5 rectangle can represent one whole.*

Journal Prompt

How do you like to solve fraction problems—using pattern blocks, rectangles on dot paper, number lines, or symbols? Tell why.

Math Facts

DPP item E provides practice with math facts involving multiplication by multiples of ten.

Homework and Practice

*   Assign the Homework section in the *Student Guide.*
*   Assign Part 2 of the Home Practice which reviews the order of operations.

Answers for Part 2 of the Home Practice are in the Answer Key at the end of this lesson and at the end of this unit.

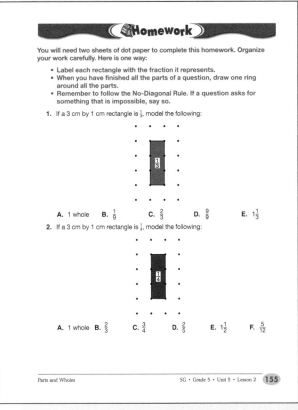

Student Guide - page 155 (Answers on p. 54)

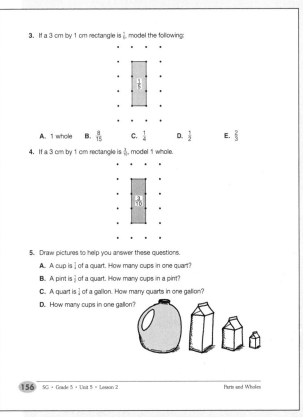

Student Guide - page 156 (Answers on p. 55)

Unit 5 **Home Practice**

PART 1 *Triangle Flash Cards: 9s*

Study for the quiz on the multiplication and division facts for the nines. Take home your *Triangle Flash Cards: 9s* and your list of facts you need to study.

Ask a family member to choose one flash card at a time. To quiz you on a multiplication fact, he or she should cover the corner containing the highest number. Multiply the two uncovered numbers.

To quiz you on a division fact, your family member can cover one of the smaller numbers. One of the smaller numbers is circled. The other has a square around it. Use the two uncovered numbers to solve a division fact.

Ask your family member to mix up the multiplication and division facts. He or she should sometimes cover the highest number, sometimes cover the circled number, and sometimes cover the number in the square.

Your teacher will tell you when the quiz on the 9s will be given.

PART 2 **Order of Operations**

Solve the following problems using the order of operations.

A. $33 - 8 \times 3 =$

B. $35 \div 7 - 3 =$

C. $150 \div 9 \times 6 =$

D. $45 \div 9 \times 4 =$

E. $100 + 200 \div 10 =$

F. $(6 + 3) \times 100 =$

G. $200 - (2 \times 70) =$

H. $60 \times 60 \div 40 =$

I. $(80 + 80) \div 40 =$

INVESTIGATING FRACTIONS   DAB • Grade 5 • Unit 5   **71**

Discovery Assignment Book - page 71 *(Answers on p. 55)*

Assessment

- Observe students as they are working in class. Record their abilities to represent fractions on the *Observational Assessment Record* and students' *Individual Assessment Record Sheets*.

- Use **Question 3** in the Homework section to assess students' abilities to model fractions using rectangles on dot paper. When given a fractional part of a whole, they model one whole and other fractional parts of the whole.

- Give a short quiz. Define one whole as a yellow hexagon and a 3×4 rectangle on dot paper. Model fractions using overhead pattern blocks and ask students to represent the same fractions using rectangles on dot paper.

Extension

Assign DPP item F that asks students to solve a problem involving averages. This problem can serve as a challenging "Problem of the Day."

Math Facts and Daily Practice and Problems

Assign DPP items E and F. Item E reviews math facts with multiples of ten. Item F is a challenging problem involving averages.

Part 1. Modeling Fractions with Pattern Blocks and Rectangles on Dot Paper

1. Model fractions on the overhead using pattern blocks and ask students to model the same fractions using rectangles on dot paper.
2. Model fractions on the overhead using rectangles on dot paper. Ask students to model the fractions with pattern blocks.
3. Students work in pairs to model fractions using pattern blocks and rectangles on dot paper for *Questions 1–3* on the *Parts and Wholes* Activity Pages in the *Student Guide.*

Part 2. Parts to Wholes with Pattern Blocks

Students complete *Questions 4–6* in the *Student Guide.* When given a fractional part of the whole, students model the whole and other fractions with pattern blocks.

Part 3. Parts to Wholes with Rectangles

Students complete *Questions 7–9.* When given a fractional part of the whole, they model the whole and other fractions with rectangles.

Homework

1. Assign the Homework section in the *Student Guide.*
2. Assign Part 2 of the Home Practice.

Assessment

1. Use *Question 3* in the Homework section to assess students' abilities to model fractions using rectangles on dot paper.
2. Give a short quiz to assess students' abilities to represent fractions using rectangles on dot paper as you model various fractions using overhead pattern blocks.
3. Record students' abilities to represent fractions on the *Observational Assessment Record.*
4. Transfer your observations to students' *Individual Assessment Record Sheets.*

Extension

Assign DPP item F.

Answer Key is on pages 52–55.

Notes:

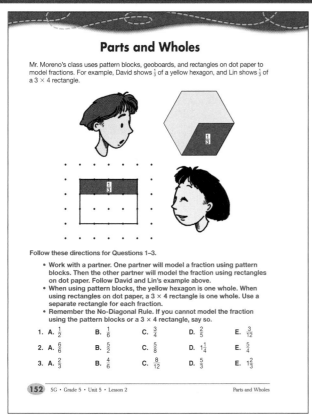

Student Guide - page 152

Student Guide (p. 152)

Answers will vary. The area of the fractional parts must be the same. One possible solution for each question is shown.

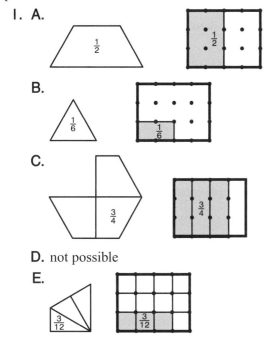

I. A.
$\frac{1}{2}$

B.
$\frac{1}{6}$

C.
$\frac{3}{4}$

D. not possible

E.
$\frac{3}{12}$

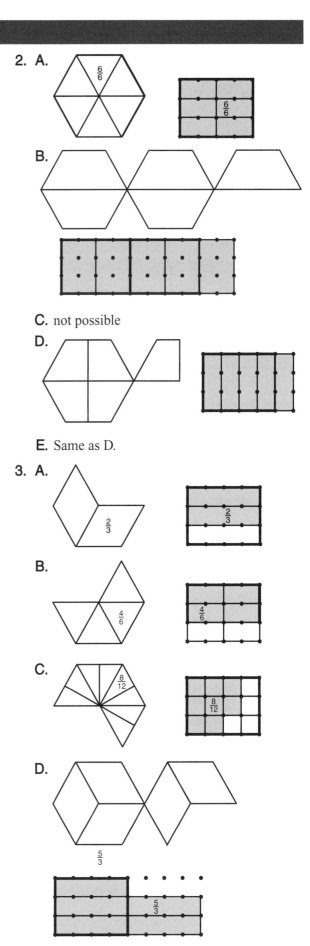

2. A.
$\frac{6}{6}$

B.

C. not possible

D.

E. Same as D.

3. A.
$\frac{2}{3}$

B.
$\frac{4}{6}$

C.
$\frac{8}{12}$

D.
$\frac{5}{3}$

E. Same as D.

Student Guide (p. 153)

4. A.

B.

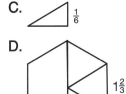

2/3

C.

1/6

D.

1 2/3

5. See Figure 11 in Lesson Guide 2.*

6. See Figure 13 in Lesson Guide 2.*

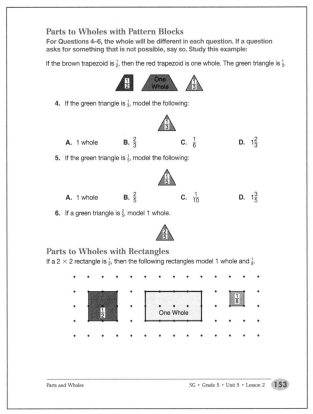

Student Guide - page 153

Student Guide (p. 154)

7. A.

One Whole

B.

2/3

C.

1/6

D.

5/3

E.

6/6

F. not possible

8. See Figure 12 in Lesson Guide 2.*

9. See Figure 14 in Lesson Guide 2.*

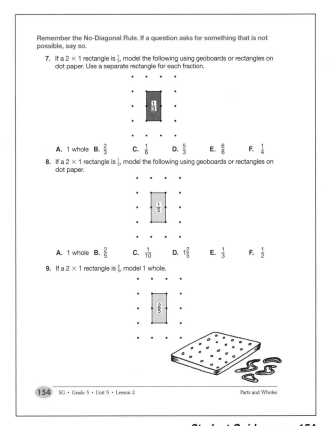

Student Guide - page 154

*Answers and/or discussion are included in the Lesson Guide.

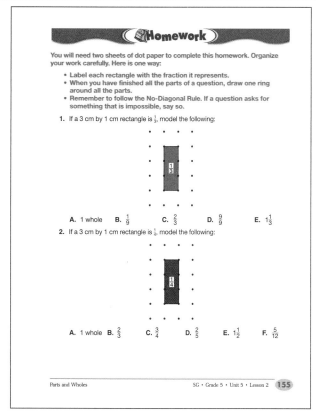

Student Guide - page 155

Student Guide (p. 155)

Homework

1. Shapes may vary. Areas must be the same as shown.

   A.

   B.

   C.

   D.

   E.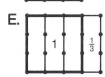

2. Shapes may vary. Areas must be the same as shown.

   A.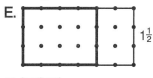

   B.

   C.

   D. not possible

   E.

   F.

Student Guide (p. 156)

3. Shapes will vary. Areas must be the same as shown.

A.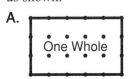

B.  $\frac{8}{15}$

C. not possible **D.** not possible

E.  $\frac{2}{3}$

4. The shapes may vary. The area must be the same as shown.

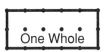

5. **A.** 4 cups **B.** 2 cups
   C. 4 quarts **D.** 16 cups

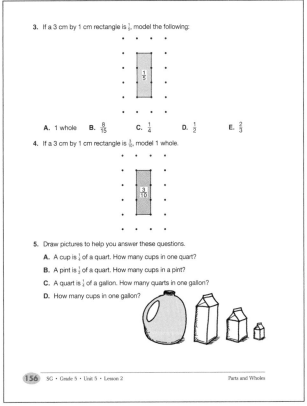

3. If a 3 cm by 1 cm rectangle is $\frac{1}{5}$, model the following:

$\frac{1}{5}$

A. 1 whole **B.** $\frac{8}{15}$ **C.** $\frac{1}{4}$ **D.** $\frac{1}{2}$ **E.** $\frac{2}{3}$

4. If a 3 cm by 1 cm rectangle is $\frac{3}{10}$, model 1 whole.

$\frac{3}{10}$

5. Draw pictures to help you answer these questions.
   A. A cup is $\frac{1}{4}$ of a quart. How many cups in one quart?
   B. A pint is $\frac{1}{2}$ of a quart. How many cups in a pint?
   C. A quart is $\frac{1}{4}$ of a gallon. How many quarts in one gallon?
   D. How many cups in one gallon?

156   SG • Grade 5 • Unit 5 • Lesson 2   Parts and Wholes

Student Guide - page 156

Discovery Assignment Book (p. 71)

Home Practice*

Part 2. Order of Operations

A. 9
B. 2
C. 204
D. 20
E. 120
F. 900
G. 60
H. 90
I. 4

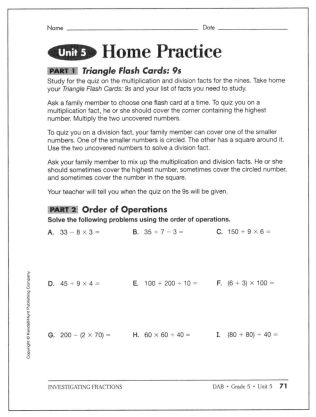

Name _____ Date _____

Unit 5 Home Practice

PART 1 *Triangle Flash Cards: 9s*
Study for the quiz on the multiplication and division facts for the nines. Take home your *Triangle Flash Cards: 9s* and your list of facts you need to study.

Ask a family member to choose one flash card at a time. To quiz you on a multiplication fact, he or she should cover the corner containing the highest number. Multiply the two uncovered numbers.

To quiz you on a division fact, your family member can cover one of the smaller numbers. One of the smaller numbers is circled. The other has a square around it. Use the two uncovered numbers to solve a division fact.

Ask your family member to mix up the multiplication and division facts. He or she should sometimes cover the highest number, sometimes cover the circled number, and sometimes cover the number in the square.

Your teacher will tell you when the quiz on the 9s will be given.

PART 2 Order of Operations
Solve the following problems using the order of operations.

A. $33 - 8 \times 3 =$ **B.** $35 \div 7 - 3 =$ **C.** $150 + 9 \times 6 =$

D. $45 \div 9 \times 4 =$ **E.** $100 + 200 \div 10 =$ **F.** $(6 + 3) \times 100 =$

G. $200 - (2 \times 70) =$ **H.** $60 \times 60 \div 40 =$ **I.** $(80 + 80) \div 40 =$

INVESTIGATING FRACTIONS   DAB • Grade 5 • Unit 5 **71**

Discovery Assignment Book - page 71

*Answers for all the Home Practice in the *Discovery Assignment Book* are at the end of the unit.

Using Dot Paper Rectangles

Lesson Overview

Estimated Class Sessions

1-2

In Part 1 students practice writing fraction sentences using dot paper rectangles in a game called *Fraction Cover-All*. In Part 2 students write equivalent fractions using dot paper rectangles. Both parts of this lesson prepare students for Lessons 4–7 in which they use common denominators to compare, add, and subtract fractions.

Key Content

- Representing fractions with pictures and symbols.
- Finding equivalent fractions.
- Writing addition and multiplication sentences with fractions.

Key Vocabulary

- equivalent fractions

Math Facts

Continue reviewing the multiplication and division facts for the 9s using *Triangle Flash Cards.*

Homework

1. Assign the Homework section in the *Student Guide.*
2. Assign the *Equivalent Fractions on Dot Paper* Activity Pages in the *Discovery Assignment Book.*
3. Assign Part 4 of the Home Practice.

Assessment

Use *Question 1* in the Homework section.

Curriculum Sequence

Before This Unit

Number Sentences with Fractions

In Unit 3 Lesson 2 students wrote addition number sentences representing figures made with pattern block fractions. In Unit 3 Lesson 3 students used number lines to help them write equivalent fractions.

After This Unit

Equivalent Fractions

In Unit 11, in their study of factors and multiples, students further explore equivalent fractions as they learn to reduce fractions.

Adding and Subtracting Fractions

In Unit 12 students develop paper-and-pencil procedures for adding and subtracting fractions.

Materials List

Supplies and Copies

Student	Teacher
Supplies for Each Student	**Supplies** • 1 set of 6 index cards with the following fractions: $\frac{1}{2}, \frac{1}{4}, \frac{1}{3}, \frac{1}{6}, \frac{1}{12}, \frac{1}{12}$
Copies • 3–4 copies of *Centimeter Dot Paper* per student (*Unit Resource Guide* Page 36)	**Copies/Transparencies** • 1 transparency of *Centimeter Dot Paper* (*Unit Resource Guide* Page 36)

All blackline masters including assessment, transparency, and DPP masters are also on the Teacher Resource CD.

Student Books

Using Dot Paper Rectangles (*Student Guide* Pages 157–159)
Equivalent Fractions on Dot Paper (*Discovery Assignment Book* Pages 77–78)

Daily Practice and Problems and Home Practice

DPP items G–H (*Unit Resource Guide* Pages 19–20)
Home Practice Part 4 (*Discovery Assignment Book* Page 73)

Note: Classrooms whose pacing differs significantly from the suggested pacing of the units should use the Math Facts Calendar in Section 4 of the *Facts Resource Guide* to ensure students receive the complete math facts program.

Daily Practice and Problems

Suggestions for using the DPPs are on page 62.

G. Bit: Subtraction Practice (URG p. 19)

Solve the following problems in your head.

A. $1000 - 1 =$	B. $300 - 29 =$
C. $1505 - 10 =$	D. $150 - 25 =$
E. $90 - 33 =$	F. $460 - 160 =$

H. Task: Making Change
(URG p. 20)

How many ways can you make change for a $50 bill using only $5 bills, $10 bills, and $20 bills?

Before the Activity

Make a set of six index cards with the numbers
$\frac{1}{2}, \frac{1}{3}, \frac{1}{4}, \frac{1}{6}, \frac{1}{12},$ and $\frac{1}{12}$ on them. See Figure 15.

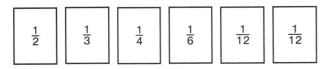

| $\frac{1}{2}$ | $\frac{1}{3}$ | $\frac{1}{4}$ | $\frac{1}{6}$ | $\frac{1}{12}$ | $\frac{1}{12}$ |

Figure 15: *Cards for* Fraction Cover-All

Teaching the Activity

Part 1 *Fraction Cover-All*

The rules for this game are on the *Using Dot Paper Rectangles* Activity Pages in the *Student Guide*. Read and discuss the rules with the class. Have them look at Ana's rectangle in the *Student Guide* (see Figure 16).

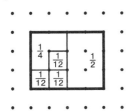

Figure 16: *Ana's game board*

Ask students, *"Are there other ways to divide the rectangle using the same fractions?"* Discuss other possible rectangles. Remind students that a fraction must be made of a continuous area. In other words, $\frac{1}{2}$ must be represented by a shape with a total continuous area of 6 square units as opposed to 6 square units that are isolated or joined only at corners.

Look at the eight number sentences that Ana wrote using her game board. Discuss **Question 1** in the *Student Guide*. The number sentence $\frac{1}{4} + \frac{1}{4} = \frac{1}{2}$, while a true sentence, is not acceptable because $\frac{1}{4}$ is represented only once on her game board. The sentence $\frac{1}{12} + \frac{1}{12} = \frac{1}{6}$ is also a true sentence; however, $\frac{1}{6}$ is not represented on Ana's board, so this sentence cannot be used. The sentence $\frac{1}{4} + \frac{1}{12} = \frac{2}{12}$ is not allowed because it is not a true sentence. **Question 2** asks students to suggest other number sentences that Ana can use. Some possible responses include:
$\frac{1}{12} + \frac{1}{12} + \frac{1}{12} + \frac{1}{4} = \frac{1}{2}; 3 \times \frac{1}{12} = \frac{1}{4}; 1 - \frac{1}{4} = \frac{3}{12} + \frac{1}{2}.$

TIMS Tip

Remind students that repeated addition can be written as multiplication: $\frac{1}{12} + \frac{1}{12} + \frac{1}{12} = 3 \times \frac{1}{12}$.

Using Dot Paper Rectangles

Fraction Cover-All

Players

This game is for any number of players.

Materials

- *Centimeter Dot Paper*
- a set of six cards with the following numbers: $\frac{1}{2}, \frac{1}{3}, \frac{1}{4}, \frac{1}{6}, \frac{1}{12}, \frac{1}{12}$

Rules

1. Your teacher or one student is the leader. The others are the players.
2. Each player draws a 3 × 4 rectangle on dot paper. The rectangle is one whole.
3. The leader shuffles the cards, takes the top card, and reads the fraction.
4. Each player draws the fraction on his or her rectangle and labels the fraction. The fraction can be any shape, but players must follow the No-Diagonal Rule. The fraction must be made of small squares connected together.
5. The leader returns the card to the deck, shuffles again, chooses a card, and reads another fraction.
6. Play continues until at least one player fills his or her rectangle completely. (If a fraction will not fit on a player's rectangle, but the rectangle is not yet filled, the player does nothing on that turn.)
7. At this point in the game, all the players try to make as many number sentences as they can using the fractions on their rectangles.
   - They may use any operation.
   - They may use whole numbers in the sentences.
   - They may only use fractions and denominators that are on their rectangles.
   - They may only use a fraction as many times as it appears on their rectangles.
8. The winner is the player with the largest number of acceptable number sentences.

Using Dot Paper Rectangles   SG • Grade 5 • Unit 5 • Lesson 3   **157**

Student Guide - page 157

Discuss

Ana played *Fraction Cover-All*. Mr. Moreno read these fractions: $\frac{1}{2}, \frac{1}{12}, \frac{1}{4}, \frac{1}{12},$ and $\frac{1}{12}$. Here are Ana's rectangle and her number sentences. She circled the sentences that were allowed.

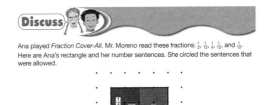

$\left(\frac{1}{4} + \frac{3}{12} + \frac{1}{2} = 1\right)$ $\left(3 \times \frac{1}{12} = \frac{3}{12}\right)$

$\left(\frac{1}{4} = \frac{3}{12}\right)$ $\frac{1}{12} + \frac{1}{12} = \frac{1}{6}$

$\frac{1}{4} + \frac{1}{4} = \frac{1}{2}$ $\frac{1}{4} + \frac{1}{12} = \frac{2}{12}$

$\left(\frac{1}{2} - \frac{1}{4} = \frac{3}{12}\right)$ $\left(1 - \frac{1}{4} - \frac{3}{12} = \frac{1}{2}\right)$

1. What is wrong with the sentences that are not circled?
2. Write more number sentences for Ana.

158   SG • Grade 5 • Unit 5 • Lesson 3   Using Dot Paper Rectangles

Student Guide - page 158 (Answers on p. 64)

Play several rounds of this game with your class. Play the game with you as the leader or in smaller groups with a student leader in each group. Rotate the job of student leader within a group after each round. One set of fraction cards will be needed for each group.

Play stops when one or more students fill their rectangles completely. Then each student writes as many acceptable sentences as possible using his or her rectangle. Impose a time limit of 1 or 2 minutes. When students finish writing sentences, identify the student or students with the most sentences. As a class, check that the student's sentences are true and follow the guidelines in Part G of the rules.

The Homework section in the *Student Guide* includes problems similar to *Fraction Cover-All*.

Part 2 **Equivalent Fractions on Dot Paper**
In Lesson 4 of this unit, students compare fractions using common denominators. They will choose a common denominator for a pair of fractions using dot paper rectangles. Part 2 of this lesson gives students practice in modeling equivalent fractions with dot paper rectangles in preparation for work in the next lesson. Students review the procedures they used in Unit 3 Lesson 3 for writing equivalent fractions.

On a transparency of *Centimeter Dot Paper*, draw a 3×5 rectangle. Ask students, *"How can I show $\frac{2}{3}$ using this rectangle?"* Have a student volunteer shade $\frac{2}{3}$. See Figure 17.

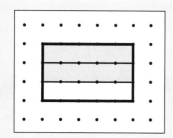

Figure 17: $\frac{2}{3}$ *of a 3 × 5 rectangle*

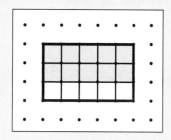

Figure 18: $\frac{2}{3} = \frac{10}{15}$

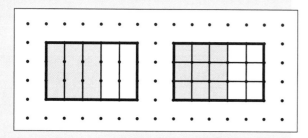

Figure 19: $\frac{3}{5} = \frac{9}{15}$

Draw in vertical lines as in Figure 18. The shaded part, $\frac{2}{3}$, is now seen as equivalent to the fraction $\frac{10}{15}$. Ask:

- *How many equal parts is the rectangle divided into now?* (15)
- *How many parts are shaded?* (10)
- *What fraction of the whole rectangle is shaded?* ($\frac{10}{15}$)
- *Two-thirds equals how many fifteenths?* ($\frac{10}{15}$)

Remind students of their work in Unit 3. Ask:

- *What number can be multiplied by the 2 and 3 in $\frac{2}{3}$ to get $\frac{10}{15}$?* (5: $\frac{2}{3} = \frac{2 \times 5}{3 \times 5} = \frac{10}{15}$)

Provide another example. Begin with a clean copy of a 3×5 rectangle. Ask a student volunteer to shade $\frac{3}{5}$ of the rectangle. Then have students write a fraction equivalent to $\frac{3}{5}$. This time, by drawing in the horizontal lines, students will see that $\frac{3}{5} = \frac{9}{15}$ (see Figure 19). Point out that if you divide both the numerator and denominator of $\frac{9}{15}$ by 3, you will get $\frac{3}{5}$: $\frac{9}{15} = \frac{9 \div 3}{15 \div 3} = \frac{3}{5}$.

Provide a third example. Begin with a 3 × 4 rectangle. Ask a student volunteer to shade $\frac{1}{3}$. Have students use the rectangle to write an equivalent fraction with a denominator of 6. One way to divide the 3 × 4 rectangle into sixths is to draw one vertical line as shown in Figure 20. This example differs from the other two in that we do not divide the rectangle into its 12 individual unit squares (we divided the rectangle into sixths instead of twelfths). A fraction equivalent to $\frac{1}{3}$ is $\frac{2}{6}$ (see Figure 20). Multiplying both the numerator and the denominator by 2 results in an equivalent fraction: $\frac{1}{3} = \frac{1 \times 2}{3 \times 2} = \frac{2}{6}$. If we further divide the rectangle into twelfths, we can obtain yet another equivalent fraction, $\frac{4}{12}$.

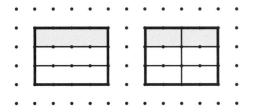

Figure 20: *Showing $\frac{1}{3} = \frac{2}{6}$ using a 3 × 4 rectangle*

Have students turn to the *Equivalent Fractions on Dot Paper* Activity Pages in the *Discovery Assignment Book.* Have them complete this activity in class or for homework.

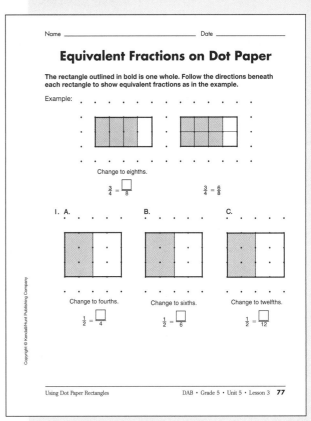

Discovery Assignment Book - page 77 (Answers on p. 66)

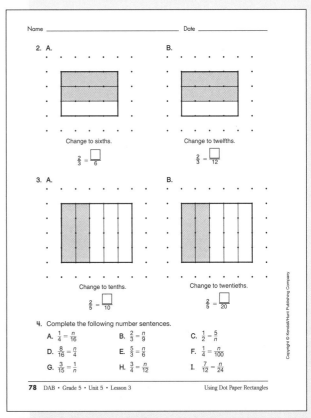

Discovery Assignment Book - page 78 (Answers on p. 66)

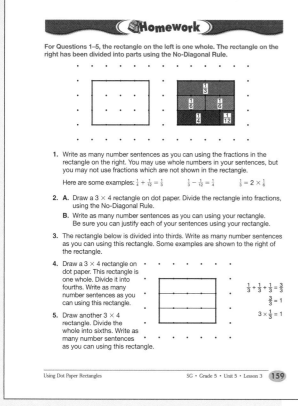

Student Guide - page 159 *(Answers on p. 64)*

Homework

For Questions 1–5, the rectangle on the left is one whole. The rectangle on the right has been divided into parts using the No-Diagonal Rule.

1. Write as many number sentences as you can using the fractions in the rectangle on the right. You may use whole numbers in your sentences, but you may not use fractions which are not shown in the rectangle.

   Here are some examples: $\frac{1}{4} + \frac{1}{12} = \frac{1}{3}$ $\frac{1}{3} - \frac{1}{12} = \frac{1}{4}$ $\frac{1}{3} = 2 \times \frac{1}{6}$

2. **A.** Draw a 3×4 rectangle on dot paper. Divide the rectangle into fractions, using the No-Diagonal Rule.

   B. Write as many number sentences as you can using your rectangle. Be sure you can justify each of your sentences using your rectangle.

3. The rectangle below is divided into thirds. Write as many number sentences as you can using this rectangle. Some examples are shown to the right of the rectangle.

4. Draw a 3×4 rectangle on dot paper. This rectangle is one whole. Divide it into fourths. Write as many number sentences as you can using this rectangle.

   $\frac{1}{3} + \frac{1}{3} + \frac{1}{3} = \frac{3}{3}$
   $\frac{3}{3} = 1$
   $3 \times \frac{1}{3} = 1$

5. Draw another 3×4 rectangle. Divide the whole into sixths. Write as many number sentences as you can using this rectangle.

Using Dot Paper Rectangles   SG • Grade 5 • Unit 5 • Lesson 3   **159**

Name _____ Date _____

PART 4 Fractions
You will need *Centimeter Dot Paper* to complete this part.

1. Complete each number sentence. Draw a picture on dot paper for each fraction. A 3×4 rectangle is one whole.

   A. $1\frac{2}{3} = \frac{n}{3}$ **B.** $2\frac{3}{4} = \frac{n}{4}$

   C. $1\frac{1}{6} = \frac{n}{6}$ **D.** $3\frac{1}{6} = \frac{n}{6}$

2. Write each mixed number as an improper fraction.

   A. $2\frac{3}{5} =$ _____   **B.** $3\frac{1}{4} =$ _____

   C. $3\frac{3}{10} =$ _____   **D.** $3\frac{5}{8} =$ _____

3. Write each improper fraction as a mixed number.

   A. $\frac{13}{6} =$ _____   **B.** $\frac{7}{2} =$ _____

   C. $\frac{10}{3} =$ _____   **D.** $\frac{14}{5} =$ _____

PART 5 Practicing the Operations

1. Solve the following problems in your head. Estimate the answers to F and G.

   A. 240 + 60 = _____ **B.** 2089 + 401 = _____ **C.** 1250 − 300 = _____

   D. 10,000 − 6700 = _____   **E.** 3800 + 1200 = _____

   F. Estimate: 89 × 18   **G.** Estimate: 1270 ÷ 50

2. Use a separate sheet of paper. Solve the following problems using a paper-and-pencil method. Estimate to be sure your answers are reasonable.

   A. 473 + 1548 = _____   **B.** 28 × 59 = _____

   C. 7034 ÷ 9 = _____   **D.** 3704 − 478 = _____

INVESTIGATING FRACTIONS   DAB • Grade 5 • Unit 5   **73**

Discovery Assignment Book - page 73 *(Answers on p. 65)*

Continue reviewing the multiplication and division facts for the 9s using *Triangle Flash Cards*.

Homework and Practice

- Assign the Homework section on the *Using Dot Paper Rectangles* Activity Pages in the *Student Guide*.

- Assign the *Equivalent Fractions on Dot Paper* Activity Pages in the *Discovery Assignment Book* for homework.

- Assign DPP items G and H for practice with computation and money.

- Assign Part 4 of the Home Practice.

Answers for Part 4 of the Home Practice are in the Answer Key at the end of this lesson and at the end of this unit.

Assessment

Use **Question 1** in the Homework section to assess students' abilities to write correct number sentences.

Extension

Play *Fraction Cover-All* with a different size rectangle and different fraction cards. For example, use a 4×6 rectangle and make cards with the following fractions: $\frac{1}{2}$, $\frac{1}{3}$, $\frac{1}{4}$, $\frac{1}{6}$, $\frac{1}{8}$, $\frac{1}{12}$, and $\frac{1}{24}$. Or use a 4×5 rectangle and make cards with the following fractions: $\frac{1}{2}$, $\frac{1}{4}$, $\frac{1}{5}$, $\frac{1}{10}$, and $\frac{1}{20}$.

At a Glance

Math Facts and Daily Practice and Problems

Complete DPP items G–H. Item G reviews mental computation with subtraction. Item H involves computation with money.

Part 1. *Fraction Cover-All*

1. Students read the rules for *Fraction Cover-All* on the *Using Dot Paper Rectangles* Activity Pages in the *Student Guide.*
2. Students discuss Ana's game board and number sentences that are in the *Student Guide.*
3. Play *Fraction Cover-All.*

Part 2. Equivalent Fractions on Dot Paper

1. Draw a 3 × 5 rectangle on a transparency of *Centimeter Dot Paper.* Have a student volunteer shade $\frac{2}{3}$ of the rectangle.
2. Ask students how you can show a fraction equivalent to $\frac{2}{3}$. Draw in the vertical lines to divide the rectangle into 15 equal pieces. The shaded part now shows $\frac{2}{3}$ or $\frac{10}{15}$.
3. Repeat with the fractions $\frac{3}{5}$ and $\frac{9}{15}$.
4. Follow the same procedure using a 3 × 4 rectangle with the fractions $\frac{1}{3}$, $\frac{2}{6}$, and $\frac{4}{12}$.
5. Read the directions and discuss the example on the *Equivalent Fractions on Dot Paper* Activity Pages in the *Discovery Assignment Book.* Students complete these pages in class or as homework.

Homework

1. Assign the Homework section in the *Student Guide.*
2. Assign the *Equivalent Fractions on Dot Paper* Activity Pages in the *Discovery Assignment Book.*
3. Assign Part 4 of the Home Practice.

Assessment

Use *Question 1* in the Homework section.

Extension

Play *Fraction Cover-All* with a different size rectangle and different fraction cards.

Answer Key is on pages 64–66.

Notes:

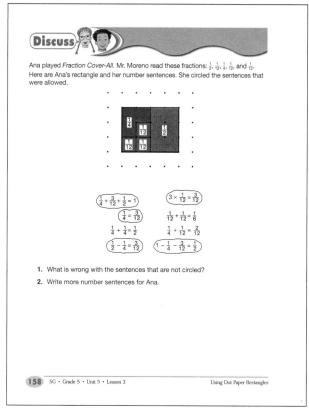

Student Guide - page 158

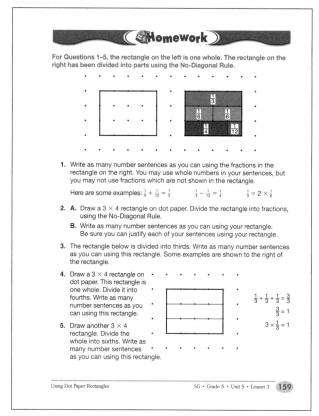

Student Guide - page 159

*Answers and/or discussion are included in the Lesson Guide.

Student Guide (p. 158)

1. $\frac{1}{4} + \frac{1}{4} = \frac{1}{2}$ is not acceptable because $\frac{1}{4}$ is represented only once on the game board. $\frac{1}{12} + \frac{1}{12} = \frac{1}{6}$ is not acceptable because $\frac{1}{6}$ is not represented on the game board. $\frac{1}{4} + \frac{1}{12} = \frac{2}{12}$ is not a true sentence.*

2. $\frac{1}{12} + \frac{1}{12} + \frac{1}{12} + \frac{1}{4} = \frac{1}{2}$; $3 \times \frac{1}{12} = \frac{1}{4}$; $1 - \frac{1}{4} = \frac{3}{12} + \frac{1}{2}$; etc.*

Student Guide (p. 159)

Homework

1. Answers will vary. Some possible answers are:
$\frac{1}{3} - \frac{1}{6} = \frac{1}{6}$; $\frac{1}{3} + \frac{2}{6} + \frac{1}{4} + \frac{1}{12} = 1$;
$1 - \frac{1}{3} - \frac{2}{6} = \frac{1}{4} + \frac{1}{12}$.

2. **A.** Answers will vary. The figure below shows one possible answer:

   B. Fraction sentences for the rectangle in 2A:
$\frac{1}{2} = \frac{4}{12} + \frac{1}{6}$; $\frac{1}{2} - \frac{1}{6} = \frac{4}{12}$; $\frac{1}{12} + \frac{1}{12} = \frac{1}{6}$

3. Answers will vary. Some possible answers are:
$1 - \frac{1}{3} = \frac{2}{3}$; $\frac{2}{3} + \frac{1}{3} = 1$

4. Answers will vary.

   Some possible number sentences are:
$\frac{1}{4} \times 4 = \frac{4}{4}$; $\frac{1}{4} + \frac{1}{4} + \frac{1}{4} + \frac{1}{4} = 1$; $\frac{4}{4} = 1$; $1 - \frac{3}{4} = \frac{1}{4}$

5. Answers will vary.

   Some possible number sentences are:
$\frac{1}{6} \times 6 = \frac{6}{6}$; $\frac{6}{6} = 1$; $\frac{1}{6} + \frac{1}{6} + \frac{1}{6} = \frac{3}{6}$

Discovery Assignment Book (p. 73)

Home Practice*

Part 4. Fractions

Shapes of fractions may vary. Area must be the same as shown.

I. A. $1\frac{2}{3} = \frac{5}{3}$

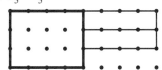

B. $2\frac{3}{4} = \frac{11}{4}$

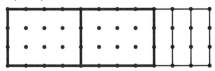

C. $1\frac{1}{6} = \frac{7}{6}$

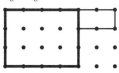

D. $3\frac{1}{6} = \frac{19}{6}$

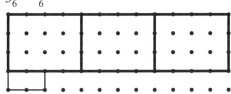

2. A. $\frac{13}{5}$

   B. $\frac{13}{4}$

   C. $\frac{33}{10}$

   D. $\frac{29}{8}$

3. A. $2\frac{1}{6}$

   B. $3\frac{1}{2}$

   C. $3\frac{1}{3}$

   D. $2\frac{4}{5}$

Name _____ Date _____

PART 4 **Fractions**
You will need *Centimeter Dot Paper* to complete this part.

1. Complete each number sentence. Draw a picture on dot paper for each fraction. A 3 × 4 rectangle is one whole.

   A. $1\frac{2}{3} = \frac{n}{3}$ B. $2\frac{3}{4} = \frac{n}{4}$

   C. $1\frac{1}{6} = \frac{n}{6}$ D. $3\frac{1}{6} = \frac{n}{6}$

2. Write each mixed number as an improper fraction.

   A. $2\frac{3}{5} =$ _____   B. $3\frac{1}{4} =$ _____

   C. $3\frac{3}{10} =$ _____   D. $3\frac{5}{8} =$ _____

3. Write each improper fraction as a mixed number.

   A. $\frac{13}{6} =$ _____   B. $\frac{7}{2} =$ _____

   C. $\frac{10}{3} =$ _____   D. $\frac{14}{5} =$ _____

PART 5 **Practicing the Operations**

1. Solve the following problems in your head. Estimate the answers to F and G.

   A. 240 + 60 = _____   B. 2089 + 401 = _____   C. 1250 − 300 = _____

   D. 10,000 − 6700 = _____   E. 3800 + 1200 = _____

   F. Estimate: 89 × 18   G. Estimate: 1270 ÷ 50

2. Use a separate sheet of paper. Solve the following problems using a paper-and-pencil method. Estimate to be sure your answers are reasonable.

   A. 473 + 1548 = _____   B. 28 × 59 = _____

   C. 7034 ÷ 9 = _____   D. 3704 − 478 = _____

INVESTIGATING FRACTIONS   DAB • Grade 5 • Unit 5   **73**

Discovery Assignment Book - page 73

---

*Answers for all the Home Practice in the *Discovery Assignment Book* are at the end of the unit.

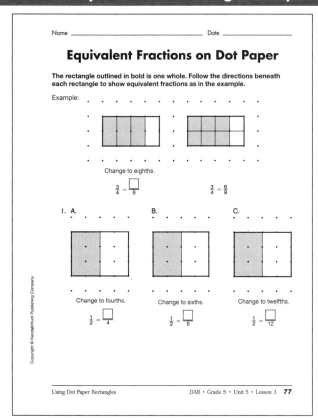

Discovery Assignment Book - page 77

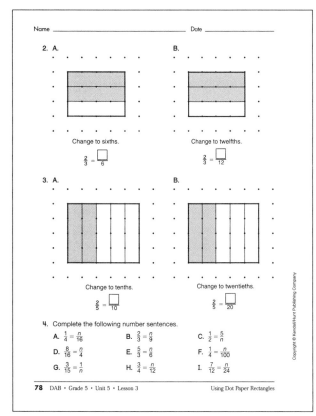

Discovery Assignment Book - page 78

Discovery Assignment Book (pp. 77–78)

Equivalent Fractions on Dot Paper

1. A.

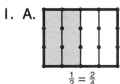

$$\frac{1}{2} = \frac{2}{4}$$

B.

$$\frac{1}{2} = \frac{3}{6}$$

C.

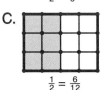

$$\frac{1}{2} = \frac{6}{12}$$

2. A.

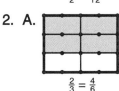

$$\frac{2}{3} = \frac{4}{6}$$

B.

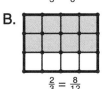

$$\frac{2}{3} = \frac{8}{12}$$

3. A.

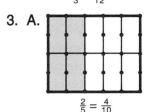

$$\frac{2}{5} = \frac{4}{10}$$

B.

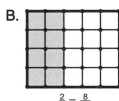

$$\frac{2}{5} = \frac{8}{20}$$

4. A. $\frac{1}{4} = \frac{4}{16}$ B. $\frac{2}{3} = \frac{6}{9}$

   C. $\frac{1}{2} = \frac{5}{10}$ D. $\frac{8}{16} = \frac{2}{4}$

   E. $\frac{5}{3} = \frac{10}{6}$ F. $\frac{1}{4} = \frac{25}{100}$

   G. $\frac{3}{15} = \frac{1}{5}$ H. $\frac{3}{4} = \frac{9}{12}$

   I. $\frac{7}{12} = \frac{14}{24}$

Lesson 4

Using Common Denominators

Estimated Class Sessions

1

Lesson Overview

Students compare fractions using common denominators. They model pairs of fractions on *Centimeter Dot Paper*. They then represent the fractions with symbols.

Key Content

- Comparing fractions using pictures and symbols.
- Finding common denominators.

Key Vocabulary

- common denominator
- denominator
- numerator

Math Facts

Complete DPP item I which uses fact families to review the multiplication and division facts for the 9s.

Homework

1. Assign *Questions 1–12* in the Homework section on the *Using Common Denominators* Activity Pages in the *Student Guide*.
2. Assign Part 5 of the Home Practice.

Assessment

Use two or three problems from the Homework section as assessment.

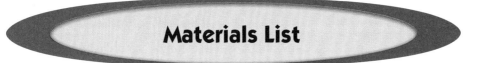

Curriculum Sequence

Before This Unit

In Unit 3 students explored patterns in equivalent fractions using pattern blocks. They also compared and ordered fractions using pattern blocks, number lines, and benchmarks such as $\frac{1}{2}$. For specific examples, see Unit 3 Lessons 3 and 4.

After This Unit

In Unit 11, as part of their study of factors and multiples, students will again use common denominators to compare fractions. In Unit 12 they will use pattern blocks to model adding and subtracting fractions and mixed numbers using common denominators.

Materials List

Supplies and Copies

Student	Teacher
Supplies for Each Student	**Supplies**
Copies • 3–4 copies of *Centimeter Dot Paper* per student (*Unit Resource Guide* Page 36)	**Copies/Transparencies** • 1 transparency of *Centimeter Dot Paper* (*Unit Resource Guide* Page 36)

All blackline masters including assessment, transparency, and DPP masters are also on the Teacher Resource CD.

Student Books

Using Common Denominators (*Student Guide* Pages 160–163)

Daily Practice and Problems and Home Practice

DPP items I–J (*Unit Resource Guide* Pages 20–21)
Home Practice Part 5 (*Discovery Assignment Book* Page 73)

Note: Classrooms whose pacing differs significantly from the suggested pacing of the units should use the Math Facts Calendar in Section 4 of the *Facts Resource Guide* to ensure students receive the complete math facts program.

Daily Practice and Problems

Suggestions for using the DPPs are on page 72.

I. Bit: Fact Families for × and ÷

(URG p. 20)

Solve each pair of related facts. Then name two other facts in the same fact family.

A. $9 \times 2 = ?$ and $18 \div 2 = ?$

B. $5 \times 9 = ?$ and $45 \div 9 = ?$

C. $7 \times 9 = ?$ and $63 \div 7 = ?$

D. $9 \times 8 = ?$ and $72 \div 9 = ?$

E. $10 \times 9 = ?$ and $90 \div 10 = ?$

F. $3 \times 9 = ?$ and $27 \div 3 = ?$

G. $9 \times 6 = ?$ and $54 \div 6 = ?$

H. $9 \times 4 = ?$ and $36 \div 9 = ?$

J. Challenge: How Many Pennies?

(URG p. 21)

1. Predict how many pennies it will take to cover your desktop. The pennies must lie flat. Record your prediction.

2. Check your prediction. (*Hint:* You don't need lots and lots of pennies. How many do you need to run across the length of your desk? How many do you need to run across the width?)

3. Is your prediction within 10% of the number you calculated in Question 2? How do you know?

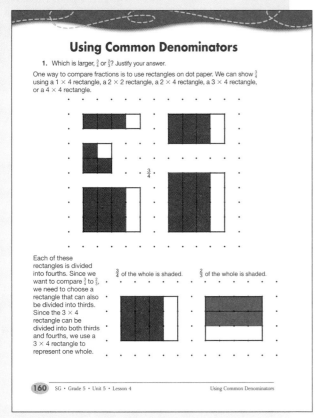

Student Guide - page 160 *(Answers on p. 74)*

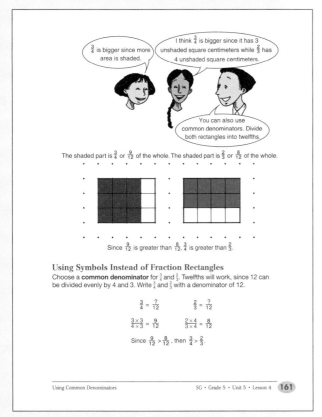

Student Guide - page 161

In Unit 3 Lesson 4 students used benchmarks to compare fractions. This is a useful strategy, but it does not always provide a clear answer about how the fractions compare with each other. This lesson explores the use of common denominators to compare fractions. As students compare fractions in this lesson, encourage them to consider various strategies. Ask:

* *Which is larger, $\frac{3}{4}$ or $\frac{2}{3}$?*

Have students discuss this question in small groups or in their journals. Encourage them to consider using benchmarks as they did in Unit 3 to compare the two fractions. Since $\frac{3}{4}$ and $\frac{2}{3}$ are both greater than $\frac{1}{2}$ and less than one, students will probably need another strategy. Ask students to share some of their ideas.

Use a transparency of *Centimeter Dot Paper* and the *Using Common Denominators* Activity Pages in the *Student Guide* to demonstrate using rectangles to compare fractions. Read the first two *Student Guide* pages. Ana and Maya look at $\frac{3}{4}$ and $\frac{2}{3}$ on their dot paper. They use different strategies to compare the fractions. Mr. Moreno suggests they divide the 3 × 4 rectangle into twelfths. Ask:

* *Why is a 3 × 4 rectangle a good size to use when comparing $\frac{3}{4}$ and $\frac{2}{3}$?* (Encourage students to think about their rectangles and use appropriate mathematical language in their responses. For example, they can say that a 3 × 4 rectangle can be divided into both thirds and fourths or that 12 can be divided evenly by 3 and 4.)

Ask students to work with a partner or in a small group to show $\frac{3}{4}$ and $\frac{2}{3}$ on dot paper (see Figure 21).

Figure 21: $\frac{3}{4}$ and $\frac{2}{3}$ on dot paper

Demonstrate dividing each rectangle into 12 parts on the overhead. See Figure 22. Ask students to do the same with their rectangles.

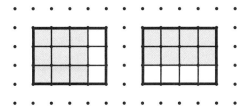

Figure 22: $\frac{9}{12}$ and $\frac{8}{12}$ on dot paper

Define 12 as a **common denominator** for $\frac{3}{4}$ and $\frac{2}{3}$ since both fractions can be written with 12 in the denominator. Ask:

- *What are the new names for the fractions?*
  $\left(\frac{3}{4} = \frac{9}{12}; \frac{2}{3} = \frac{8}{12}\right)$
- *Which fraction is larger? How can you tell?*
  (Since $\frac{9}{12}$ is greater than $\frac{8}{12}$, $\frac{3}{4}$ is greater than $\frac{2}{3}$.)

Ask, *Are there other rectangles that will work when comparing $\frac{3}{4}$ and $\frac{2}{3}$? Remember the no-diagonal rule.* Have students explore rectangles of other sizes and then list ones that work and ones that do not work. Have students draw conclusions as to why some rectangles work (e.g., 3×8, 6×4, 12×2, and 24×1) and others do not.

Once students are comfortable using rectangles to compare fractions, review the use of symbols for comparing fractions as outlined in the *Student Guide.* Show students how to rename $\frac{3}{4}$ as $\frac{9}{12}$ by multiplying both the numerator and denominator of $\frac{3}{4}$ by 3. Rename $\frac{2}{3}$ as $\frac{8}{12}$ by multiplying the numerator and denominator of $\frac{2}{3}$ by 4. By comparing the numerators of the two fractions, students should realize that $\frac{9}{12}$ is greater than $\frac{8}{12}$ and, therefore, $\frac{3}{4}$ is greater than $\frac{2}{3}$.

Questions 2–6 provide additional practice in comparing fractions. In *Questions 2–3,* students are asked to use rectangles on dot paper to compare fractions. Students then write a number sentence comparing the original fractions. In *Question 4,* students may use symbols to find a common denominator or solve the problem by again drawing rectangles on dot paper.

Explore

2. Compare $\frac{4}{5}$ and $\frac{3}{4}$.
   A. Choose a dot paper rectangle for one whole that can be divided into fourths and fifths. Draw that rectangle twice on a piece of dot paper. Show $\frac{4}{5}$ and $\frac{3}{4}$ using these rectangles.
   B. Use your rectangles to write fractions equivalent to $\frac{4}{5}$ and $\frac{3}{4}$ with a common denominator.
   C. Write a number sentence to compare $\frac{4}{5}$ and $\frac{3}{4}$.

3. Compare $\frac{3}{4}$ and $\frac{5}{6}$.
   A. Choose a dot paper rectangle for one whole that can be divided both into fourths and sixths. Draw that rectangle twice on a piece of dot paper. Show $\frac{3}{4}$ and $\frac{5}{6}$ using these rectangles.
   B. Use your rectangles to write fractions equivalent to $\frac{3}{4}$ and $\frac{5}{6}$ with a common denominator.
   C. Write a number sentence to compare $\frac{3}{4}$ and $\frac{5}{6}$.

4. Compare $\frac{2}{3}$ and $\frac{3}{5}$.
   A. Find a common denominator for $\frac{2}{3}$ and $\frac{3}{5}$. Use that denominator to write fractions equivalent to $\frac{2}{3}$ and $\frac{3}{5}$.
   B. Write a number sentence to compare $\frac{2}{3}$ and $\frac{3}{5}$.

5. Write number sentences to compare the following pairs of fractions. Try different strategies. Be prepared to share your strategies.
   A. $\frac{1}{4}, \frac{7}{10}$ B. $\frac{9}{10}, \frac{9}{12}$ C. $\frac{7}{10}, \frac{3}{5}$
   D. $\frac{1}{4}, \frac{1}{5}$ E. $\frac{7}{8}, \frac{6}{5}$ F. $\frac{5}{8}, \frac{11}{12}$

6. Place these fractions in order from smallest to largest: $\frac{11}{10}, \frac{5}{6}, \frac{2}{3}, \frac{1}{12}$. Explain your strategies.

Student Guide - page 162 (Answers on p. 74)

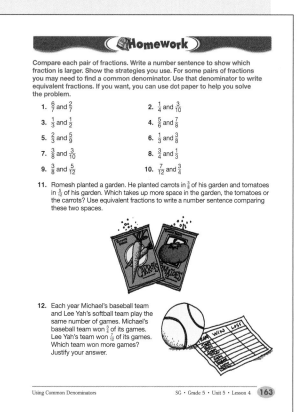

Homework

Compare each pair of fractions. Write a number sentence to show which fraction is larger. Show the strategies you use. For some pairs of fractions you may need to find a common denominator. Use that denominator to write equivalent fractions. If you want, you can use dot paper to help you solve the problem.

1. $\frac{6}{7}$ and $\frac{2}{7}$
2. $\frac{1}{4}$ and $\frac{3}{10}$
3. $\frac{1}{3}$ and $\frac{1}{2}$
4. $\frac{5}{6}$ and $\frac{7}{8}$
5. $\frac{2}{3}$ and $\frac{5}{9}$
6. $\frac{1}{3}$ and $\frac{3}{8}$
7. $\frac{3}{8}$ and $\frac{3}{10}$
8. $\frac{3}{4}$ and $\frac{1}{3}$
9. $\frac{3}{8}$ and $\frac{5}{12}$
10. $\frac{7}{12}$ and $\frac{3}{4}$

11. Romesh planted a garden. He planted carrots in $\frac{3}{8}$ of his garden and tomatoes in $\frac{5}{12}$ of his garden. Which takes up more space in the garden, the tomatoes or the carrots? Use equivalent fractions to write a number sentence comparing these two spaces.

12. Each year Michael's baseball team and Lee Yah's softball team play the same number of games. Michael's baseball team won $\frac{3}{5}$ of its games. Lee Yah's team won $\frac{7}{12}$ of its games. Which team won more games? Justify your answer.

Using Common Denominators   SG • Grade 5 • Unit 5 • Lesson 4   **163**

Student Guide - page 163 *(Answers on p. 75)*

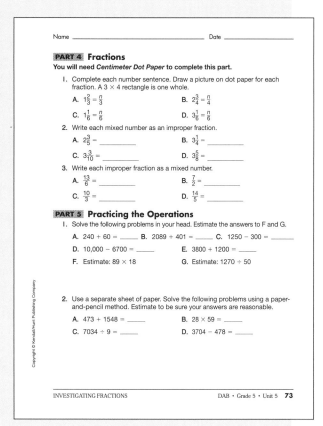

Name _____ Date _____

PART 4 Fractions
You will need *Centimeter Dot Paper* to complete this part.

1. Complete each number sentence. Draw a picture on dot paper for each fraction. A 3 × 4 rectangle is one whole.

   A. $1\frac{2}{3} = \frac{n}{3}$
   B. $2\frac{3}{4} = \frac{n}{4}$
   C. $1\frac{1}{6} = \frac{n}{6}$
   D. $3\frac{1}{6} = \frac{n}{6}$

2. Write each mixed number as an improper fraction.

   A. $2\frac{3}{5} =$ _____
   B. $3\frac{1}{4} =$ _____
   C. $3\frac{3}{10} =$ _____
   D. $3\frac{5}{8} =$ _____

3. Write each improper fraction as a mixed number.

   A. $\frac{13}{6} =$ _____
   B. $\frac{7}{2} =$ _____
   C. $\frac{10}{3} =$ _____
   D. $\frac{14}{5} =$ _____

PART 5 Practicing the Operations

1. Solve the following problems in your head. Estimate the answers to F and G.

   A. $240 + 60 =$ _____
   B. $2089 + 401 =$ _____
   C. $1250 - 300 =$ _____
   D. $10{,}000 - 6700 =$ _____
   E. $3800 + 1200 =$ _____
   F. Estimate: 89×18
   G. Estimate: $1270 \div 50$

2. Use a separate sheet of paper. Solve the following problems using a paper-and-pencil method. Estimate to be sure your answers are reasonable.

   A. $473 + 1548 =$ _____
   B. $28 \times 59 =$ _____
   C. $7034 \div 9 =$ _____
   D. $3704 - 478 =$ _____

INVESTIGATING FRACTIONS   DAB • Grade 5 • Unit 5   **73**

Copyright © Kendall/Hunt Publishing Company

Discovery Assignment Book - page 73 *(Answers on p. 75)*

Question 5 asks students to compare their pairs of fractions using different strategies. For example, although students can use common denominators to compare $\frac{1}{4}$ and $\frac{7}{10}$, it is probably more efficient to use $\frac{1}{2}$ as a benchmark. Since $\frac{1}{4}$ is less than $\frac{1}{2}$ and $\frac{7}{10}$ is greater than $\frac{1}{2}$, $\frac{1}{4} < \frac{7}{10}$. As students share their strategies for each pair of fractions, discuss the efficiency of each method. Students may work independently or in small groups to complete these problems.

TIMS Tip

Encourage students to try different strategies and to select efficient methods based on the problems. Discourage them from using one procedure for all the problems.

Content Note

Comparing Fractions. Students may not always choose the lowest common denominator when comparing fractions. As long as they are able to compare the fractions accurately and efficiently, a common denominator is all that is needed.

Math Facts

Use DPP item I to review fact families for the 9s.

Homework and Practice

- Assign homework ***Questions 1–12.*** Encourage students to choose efficient strategies to make their comparisons.
- Assign Part 5 of the Home Practice for practice with operations.

Answers for Part 5 of the Home Practice are in the Answer Key at the end of this lesson and at the end of this unit.

Assessment

Choose two or three problems from the homework to use as assessment.

Extension

Assign DPP Challenge J which involves estimation, measurement, and number sense.

At a Glance

Math Facts and Daily Practice and Problems

Complete DPP item I, which uses fact families to review the multiplication and division facts for the 9s. DPP Challenge J involves making and testing a prediction.

Teaching the Activity

1. Review the use of 0, $\frac{1}{2}$, and 1 as benchmarks for comparing fractions.
2. Ask which is larger, $\frac{3}{4}$ or $\frac{2}{3}$.
3. Discuss the need for strategies other than using benchmarks for comparing fractions. Read the first two pages of the *Using Common Denominators* Activity Pages in the *Student Guide.*
4. Use rectangles on dot paper to compare two fractions by finding a common denominator.
5. Use symbols to compare two fractions by finding a common denominator.
6. Students practice using rectangles to compare two fractions. *(Questions 2–3)*
7. Students practice using symbols to compare two fractions. *(Question 4)*
8. Students compare pairs of fractions using different strategies. *(Questions 5–6)*

Homework

1. Assign *Questions 1–12* in the Homework section on the *Using Common Denominators* Activity Pages in the *Student Guide.*
2. Assign Part 5 of the Home Practice.

Assessment

Use two or three problems from the Homework section as assessment.

Extension

Assign DPP Challenge J.

Answer Key is on pages 74–75.

Notes:

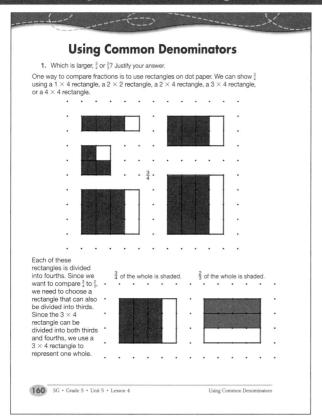

Student Guide - page 160

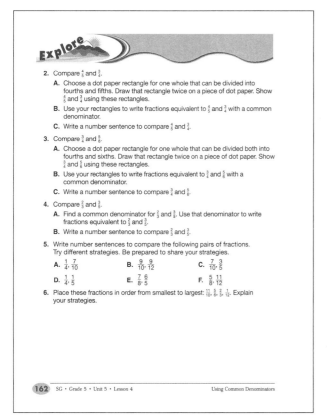

Student Guide - page 162

Student Guide (pp. 160, 162)

1.*

2. A.–B.

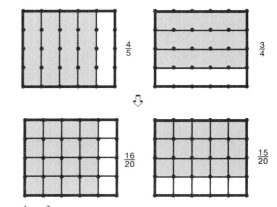

C. $\frac{4}{5} > \frac{3}{4}$

3. A.–B.

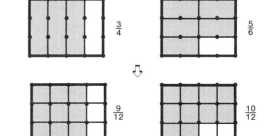

C. $\frac{3}{4} < \frac{5}{6}$

4. A. $\frac{2}{3} = \frac{10}{15}; \frac{3}{5} = \frac{9}{15}$

B. $\frac{2}{3} > \frac{3}{5}$

5. A. $\frac{1}{4} < \frac{7}{10}$*

B. $\frac{9}{10} > \frac{9}{12}$

C. $\frac{7}{10} > \frac{3}{5}$

D. $\frac{1}{4} > \frac{1}{5}$

E. $\frac{7}{8} < \frac{6}{5}$

F. $\frac{5}{8} < \frac{11}{12}$

6. $\frac{1}{12}, \frac{2}{3}, \frac{5}{6}, \frac{11}{10}$

Possible response: $\frac{1}{12}$ is the smallest because it is close to zero and less than $\frac{1}{2}$. All the other fractions are greater than $\frac{1}{2}$; $\frac{11}{10}$ is the largest because it is greater than one. All the other fractions are less than one; $\frac{2}{3} < \frac{5}{6}$, since $\frac{2}{3} = \frac{4}{6}$ and $\frac{4}{6} < \frac{5}{6}$.

*Answers and/or discussion are included in the Lesson Guide.

Student Guide (p. 163)

Homework

1. $\frac{6}{7} > \frac{2}{7}$

2. $\frac{1}{4} < \frac{3}{10}$

3. $\frac{1}{3} < \frac{1}{2}$

4. $\frac{5}{6} < \frac{7}{8}$

5. $\frac{2}{3} > \frac{5}{9}$

6. $\frac{1}{3} < \frac{3}{8}$

7. $\frac{3}{8} > \frac{3}{10}$

8. $\frac{3}{4} > \frac{1}{3}$

9. $\frac{3}{8} < \frac{5}{12}$

10. $\frac{7}{12} < \frac{3}{4}$

11. tomatoes; $\frac{3}{8} < \frac{5}{12}$; $\frac{3}{8} = \frac{9}{24}$ and $\frac{5}{12} = \frac{10}{24}$, $\frac{9}{24} < \frac{10}{24}$

12. Michael's team; $\frac{3}{4} > \frac{7}{12}$; $\frac{3}{4} = \frac{9}{12}$; $\frac{9}{12} > \frac{7}{12}$

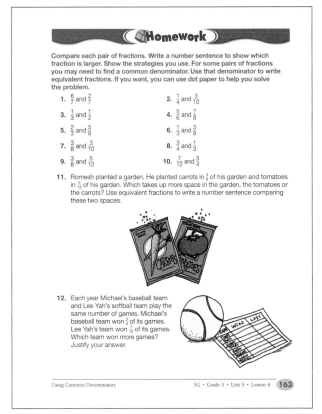

Student Guide - page 163

Discovery Assignment Book (p. 73)

Home Practice*

Part 5. Practicing the Operations

1. **A.** 300

   B. 2490

   C. 950

   D. 3300

   E. 5000

   F. Estimates will vary. One possible estimate is: $90 \times 20 = 1800$.

   G. Estimates will vary. One possible estimate is: $1250 \div 50 = 25$.

2. **A.** 2021

   B. 1652

   C. 781 R5

   D. 3226

Discovery Assignment Book - page 73

*Answers for all the Home Practice in the *Discovery Assignment Book* are at the end of the unit.

Lesson 5

A Day at the Races

Lesson Overview

Estimated Class Sessions 3-4

Students compare the speeds of their classmates as they participate in different activities: running, walking, walking backward, crawling, etc. They conduct two experiments. In Experiment 1: Six-Yard Race, each person travels for six yards and measures the time it takes. In Experiment 2: Three-Second Race, each person travels for three seconds and measures the distance traveled. They express the speeds as ratios using data tables, graphs, and fractions.

Key Content

- Using numerical variables
- Measuring length in yar
- Averaging: choosing t'
- Using ratios to solve
- Drawing and inter
- Using the steepn
- Translating bet events.
- Collecting, data.

Ma

Comp

ide.

ework.

1. Assign ʜ   ʲ the lab to determine a grade.
2. Use *Question*   bilities to draw a graph. Use *Questions 19–20* to assess the students' abilities ᴜ   ɪnd communicate solutions.
3. Use the *Observational Aₛ*   *Record* and the Assessment Indicators to record students' skills in measuring length.

Key Vocabulary

- speed
- ᵉ   ʲᶜity

Curriculum Sequence

Before This Unit

In Unit 3 *Fractions and Ratios,* the lab *Distance vs. Time* provided background for this lab. Students explored using data tables, graphs, and fractions to represent ratios in Unit 3 Lesson 5 *Using Ratios.*

After This Unit

Students will use the concepts they learned in this lab to complete similar labs such as *Mass vs. Volume* in Unit 13 and *Bats* in Unit 16.

Materials List

Supplies and Copies

Student	Teacher
Supplies for Each Student Group • 1–2 metersticks • 1–2 stopwatches • chalk or tape	**Supplies**
Copies • 2–3 copies of *Centimeter Graph Paper* or *Half-Centimeter Graph Paper* per student (*Unit Resource Guide* Pages 89–90) • 2 copies of *Three-trial Data Table* per student (*Unit Resource Guide* Page 91) • 3 copies of *Five-column Data Table* URG Page 92 per student group, optional	**Copies/Transparencies** • 1 transparency of *Centimeter Graph Paper* or *Half-Centimeter Graph Paper,* optional (*Unit Resource Guide* Pages 89–90) • 1 copy of *TIMS Multidimensional Rubric* (*Teacher Implementation Guide,* Assessment section)

All blackline masters including assessment, transparency, and DPP masters are also on the Teacher Resource CD.

Student Books

A Day at the Races (*Student Guide* Pages 164–170)
Student Rubric: *Telling* (*Student Guide* Appendix C and Inside Back Cover), optional

Daily Practice and Problems and Home Practice

DPP items K–P (*Unit Resource Guide* Pages 21–23)
Home Practice Part 3 (*Discovery Assignment Book* Page 72)

Note: Classrooms whose pacing differs significantly from the suggested pacing of the units should use the Math Facts Calendar in Section 4 of the *Facts Resource Guide* to ensure students receive the complete math facts program.

Assessment Tools

Observational Assessment Record (*Unit Resource Guide* Pages 13–14)
TIMS Multidimensional Rubric (*Teacher Implementation Guide,* Assessment section)

Daily Practice and Problems

Suggestions for using the DPPs are on pages 86–87.

K. Bit: Fact Families for × and ÷
(URG p. 21)

Complete the number sentences for the related facts.

A. $9 \times 2 =$ ___ B. $8 \times 9 =$ ___

___ $\div 9 =$ ___   ___ $\div$ ___ $= 8$

___ $\div 2 =$ ___   ___ $\div 8 =$ ___

$2 \times$ ___ $=$ ___   ___ $\times 8 =$ ___

C. $36 \div 4 =$ ___ D. $10 \times$ ___ $= 90$

___ $\times 4 =$ ___ $90 \div$ ___ $=$ ___

$36 \div$ ___ $=$ ___ $90 \div$ ___ $=$ ___

$4 \times$ ___ $=$ ___   ___ $\times 10 =$ ___

L. Challenge: Dot Paper Fractions
(URG p. 22)

If a 2 cm by 3 cm rectangle is $\frac{3}{4}$, show one whole using rectangles on dot paper.

$\cdot \ \frac{3}{4} \ \cdot$

M. Bit: Division (URG p. 22)

Use a paper-and-pencil method to solve the following. Estimate to make sure your answers make sense.

A. $2718 \div 9 =$ B. $8672 \div 9 =$

C. $7348 \div 9 =$ D. $4977 \div 9 =$

N. Task: Let's Practice (URG p. 22)

1. Solve the following problems using paper and pencil only. Estimate to make sure your answers are reasonable.

   A. $18 \times 63 =$

   B. $565 + 739 =$

   C. $2706 - 1187 =$

   D. $37 \times 29 =$

   E. $5170 \div 5 =$

   F. $17{,}235 \div 9 =$

2. List the answers in order from smallest to largest.

O. Bit: Fact Families for × and ÷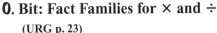
(URG p. 23)

Complete the number sentences for the related facts.

A. $3 \times 9 =$ ___ B. $9 \times 7 =$ ___

___ $\div 3 =$ ___   ___ $\div 7 =$ ___

___ $\div 9 =$ ___   ___ $\div 9 =$ ___

___ $\times 3 =$ ___ $7 \times$ ___ $=$ ___

C. $9 \times 9 =$ ___ D. $54 \div 6 =$ ___

___ $\div 9 =$ ___   ___ $\times 6 =$ ___

                        $54 \div$ ___ $=$ ___

                        ___ $\times 9 =$ ___

E. $9 \times 5 =$ ___

___ $\div 9 =$ ___

___ $\div 5 =$ ___

___ $\times 9 =$ ___

P. Challenge: The Backward Race
(URG p. 23)

Jackie's speed in the Backward Race was $\frac{18 \text{ feet}}{2.5 \text{ seconds.}}$. If she can travel at this same rate for 1 hour, how many feet will Jackie travel? How many yards is this?

A Day at the Races

On Olympic Day at Bessie Coleman School, students participated in many events, including the Sack Race and the Backward Race. Roberto and Edward entered the Sack Race. Alexis and Jackie entered the Backward Race.

Contestants in the sack race took turns hopping along the track in a large cloth sack. They hopped for three seconds. Then the racing judge measured the distance each person hopped. Roberto hopped 24 feet and Edward hopped 27 feet.

1. A. Who moved along the track faster, Edward or Roberto? How do you know?
   B. What variables are involved in the Sack Race?
   C. What variables did students measure?
   D. Which variable was the same for all the participants in the Sack Race?

The Backward Race was different. In this race, contestants tried to run or walk backward in a straight line for six yards. Alexis took 4 seconds to travel the 6 yards from the starting line to the finish line. Jackie crossed the finish line after 2.5 seconds.

2. A. Who traveled faster, Jackie or Alexis? How do you know?
   B. What variables are involved in the Backward Race?
   C. What variables did the students measure?
   D. Which variable was the same for all the participants in the Backward Race?

Student Guide - page 164 *(Answers on p. 93)*

3. A. What variable is Roberto comparing?
   B. What variable is Jackie comparing?
4. What variables do Jackie and Roberto need to consider to decide who went faster?

Speed and Velocity

To find out how fast someone or something is moving, we measure speed. To compare speeds, you need to consider both time and distance. **Speed** is the ratio of distance traveled to time taken. **Velocity** is speed in a certain direction. For example, Roberto's speed can be written $\frac{24 \text{ ft}}{3 \text{ sec}}$ which is equal to $\frac{8 \text{ ft}}{s}$. This is called a unit ratio and we write $\frac{8 \text{ ft}}{s}$. (We read $\frac{8 \text{ ft}}{s}$ as "eight feet per second.")

You are going to conduct two experiments. In each experiment, you will investigate different ways to compare the speeds of contestants in events like the Backward Race and the Sack Race.

Experiment 1: Six-Yard Race

Work in a group of four or five students. Lay out a straight track that measures 6 yards (18 ft). Each person chooses a different way of traveling down the track: running, walking backward, hopping, crawling, etc. As each person travels down the track, another person uses a stopwatch to find the time it takes to go 6 yards. Record your data in a table.

Student Guide - page 165 *(Answers on p. 93)*

Part 1   Speed and Velocity

The *A Day at the Races* Lab Pages in the *Student Guide* develop the context of the lab. *Questions 1–4* discuss the important variables. Students read about Olympic Day at Bessie Coleman School, comparing two kinds of races. In the Sack Race, students hop in a sack for three seconds and measure the distance traveled. In the Backward Race, students walk backward for six yards and measure the time it took to get from the starting line to the finish line. The variables in both races include time, distance, and speed *(Questions 1B and 2B).* To find out who traveled faster in each race, students must measure both time and distance *(Questions 1C and 2C).* However, in the sack race time is held constant *(Question 1D),* and in the Backward Race, the distance the participants walk is the same *(Question 2D).*

Questions 3–4 help students understand that speed is determined by two variables. To compare speeds, it is necessary to measure and compare both distance and time.

Content Note

Speed and Velocity. Though we use the terms interchangeably here, technically scientists distinguish between speed and velocity. **Speed** is the ratio of distance traveled to the time taken to travel that distance: distance traveled/time taken. The distances in students' races are measured in a straight line from the starting point to the finish regardless of the path the students followed. **Velocity** is speed in a certain direction.

To learn to compare speeds, students complete two experiments described in the *Student Guide*. In the first experiment, The Six-Yard Race, they choose an activity (walking, running, hopping, crawling, etc.), move for a fixed distance, and measure the time it took to travel from start to finish. Since the distance is fixed, they can compare speeds by comparing times. The shorter the time, the greater the speed. If the speeds are written as fractions, students can compare speeds by comparing fractions with common numerators. For example, using the data in the *Student Guide* for the Backward Race, we do not need to compute to see that Jackie traveled faster than Alexis:

$$\frac{6 \text{ yds}}{2.5 \text{ s}} > \frac{6 \text{ yds}}{4 \text{ s}}$$

In the other experiment, The Three-Second Sack Race, the time is held fixed and the distance traveled is measured. To compare speeds, students need only compare distances. The longer the distance the greater the speed. For example, Edward's speed was greater than Roberto's in the Sack Race:

$$\frac{27 \text{ ft}}{3 \text{ s}} > \frac{24 \text{ ft}}{3 \text{ s}}$$

Part 2 Experiment 1: Six-Yard Race

For each experiment, students will follow the four steps of the TIMS Laboratory Method: Draw, Collect, Graph, and Explore. The questions at the end of the lab will help students compare speeds when neither time nor distance is held constant. They can work in groups of four or five so they can collect data to compare four or five speeds.

The *Student Guide* describes the experimental setup shown in the picture in Figure 23. Students within each group should choose some faster activities such as running and walking forward and some slower activities such as crawling and walking backward so the differences in the times will be relatively large.

Figure 23: *Drawing of Experiment 1: Six-Yard Race*

To ensure consistent data, groups should develop and practice a uniform procedure for timing each student as he or she moves down the track. One possible procedure employs one team member posted at the starting line and a person operating the stopwatch at the finish line. A third student begins his or her chosen activity behind the starting line and moves at a steady pace past the starting line, along the track, and past the finish line. The student at the starting line says, "Start," when the participant's front foot crosses the starting line. The timer starts the stopwatch and stops it when the participant's front foot crosses the finish line.

5. Draw a picture of Experiment 1. Label the variables.

Before collecting the data, discuss the following with your group:
- The distance is the same for each participant. What other variables (or procedures) should stay the same?
- Each participant should try to travel at a constant speed. Where should each person start so that he or she moves at a steady pace for the whole six yards?
- How many trials should you time for each participant?
- If you conduct more than one trial, will you find the median or mean to average the data?
- Decide how your group will organize your data. (*Hint:* You need to record the name and activity for each participant, the time for each trial, and the average time of all the trials.)

6. Collect and record the data in a table. (You may use a *Three-trial Data Table.*)

Use your data from Question 6 to complete a new data table like the one shown below. (You may use a *Five-column Data Table.*) Write each speed as a fraction of distance over time ($\frac{D}{t}$). Note that the units are feet per second ($\frac{\text{ft}}{\text{s}}$). For example, if Jackie were in your group, her speed would be written $\frac{18 \text{ ft}}{2.5 \text{ s}}$.

Experiment 1: Six-Yard Race

Name	Activity	*D* Distance in _____	*t* Average Time in _____	*S* in ft/s Speed in Feet per Second

7. What are the measurements for time and distance when each student crosses the starting line?

166 SG • Grade 5 • Unit 5 • Lesson 5   A Day at the Races

Student Guide - page 166 *(Answers on p. 94)*

Discuss the number of trials each participant should do. While it is possible to complete the experiment with each person only moving down the track once, some experimental error is inevitable, so multiple trials will result in more accurate data. Remind students to check their data to see if their results are reasonable. If one trial is much different from the others, they should repeat the trial. Following the *Student Guide* advice to organize their data *(Question 6),* they can organize it in a *Three-trial Data Table.* See Figure 24. Note that in this example, students use the median value for the average.

Following instructions in the *Student Guide,* students transfer the information in the data table in Figure 24 to a *Five-column Data Table,* as in Figure 25. (Or, students copy this table onto their own paper using a sample in the *Student Guide.*) Students record each speed as a ratio as in Figure 25.

(Note: If your class chooses to do only one trial, record the data directly into this table and it is the only table needed.)

Encourage students to study the data in the tables. Ask, *"Who moved fastest? Who moved slowest? How can you tell?"*

Graphing the data as described in the *Student Guide* will give students another tool to compare speeds *(Question 8). Question 7* asks for the values for distance and time as each student crosses the starting line. Since the stopwatch reads 0 seconds when each student crosses the starting line at 0 feet, this point makes sense for each participant. Remind students that when they graphed distance and time for students walking at a constant speed in the lab *Distance vs. Time* in Unit 3, the data points formed a straight line. As long as students move at a steady pace in this lab, we can assume that the data fall on a

Experiment 1: Six-Yard Race

Name and Activity	t Time in Seconds			
	Trial 1	Trial 2	Trial 3	Median
John Running	2.33	2.12	2.45	2.33
Nila Crawling	11.05	10.25	10.18	10.25
Jessie Walking Backward	4.24	5.06	4.64	4.64
Arti Walking	3.23	3.40	4.22	3.40

Figure 24: *Organizing the data from three trials and recording the average time*

Experiment 1: Six-Yard Race

Name	Activity	D Distance in *feet*	t Average Time in *seconds*	S in ft/s Speed in Feet per Second
John	Running	18	2.33	18 ft/2.33 s
Nila	Crawling	18	10.25	18 ft/10.25 s
Jessie	Walking Backward	18	4.64	18 ft/4.64 s
Arti	Walking	18	3.40	18 ft/3.40 s

Figure 25: *Recording speeds for each member of the group as a fraction*

straight line. So one point is plotted for each student's data and connected by a straight line to $t = 0$ seconds and $D = 0$ feet. See Figure 26.

Experiment 1: Six-Yard Race

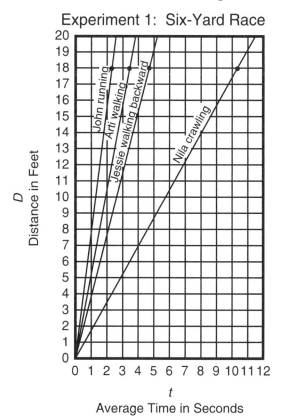

Figure 26: *Students can use the lines to compare speeds.*

Questions 9–10 in the Explore section for Experiment 1 discuss the variables in the experiment. Time, distance, speed, and the activity each student chooses (e.g., running) are all important variables. Time and distance are measured in the experiment and these two variables determine speed. *Questions 11–12* ask students to compare the speeds and describe methods for making the comparisons. Using the data table, students can compare the fractions easily since the numerators are the same. See Figure 25. John took the shortest time to cover the 6 yards, so he moved the fastest. Nila took the longest time, so she moved the slowest. Using the graph, the steeper the line, the greater the speed.

Content Note

Graphing Speeds. When graphing lines to represent speeds, time is customarily graphed on the horizontal axis and distance is graphed on the vertical axis. This way you can use the slopes or steepness of the lines to compare speeds—the greater the slope, the greater the speed.

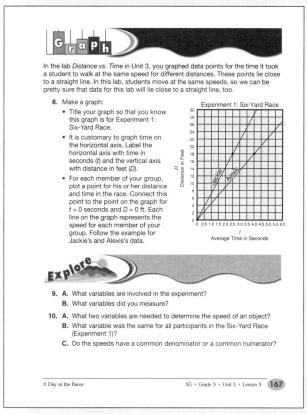

In the lab *Distance vs. Time* in Unit 3, you graphed data points for the time it took a student to walk at the same speed for different distances. These points lie close to a straight line. In this lab, students move at the same speeds, so we can be pretty sure that data for this lab will lie close to a straight line, too.

8. Make a graph:
   - Title your graph so that you know this graph is for Experiment 1: Six-Yard Race.
   - It is customary to graph time on the horizontal axis. Label the horizontal axis with time in seconds (t) and the vertical axis with distance in feet (D).
   - For each member of your group, plot a point for his or her distance and time in the race. Connect this point to the point on the graph for $t = 0$ seconds and $D = 0$ ft. Each line on the graph represents the speed for each member of your group. Follow the example for Jackie's and Alexis's data.

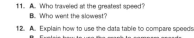

9. **A.** What variables are involved in the experiment?
   B. What variables did you measure?
10. **A.** What two variables are needed to determine the speed of an object?
    B. What variable was the same for all participants in the Six-Yard Race (Experiment 1)?
    C. Do the speeds have a common denominator or a common numerator?

A Day at the Races   SG • Grade 5 • Unit 5 • Lesson 5   **167**

Student Guide - page 167 (Answers on p. 94)

11. **A.** Who traveled at the greatest speed?
    B. Who went the slowest?
12. **A.** Explain how to use the data table to compare speeds.
    B. Explain how to use the graph to compare speeds.

Experiment 2: Three-Second Race

Work with the same group of students. Use the same activities as before, but each person should choose a different way of moving. (For example, if you crawled in the Six-Yard Race, you should not crawl in the Three-Second Race.) For this experiment, each person travels for 3 seconds. Another member of the group measures the distance traveled in feet.

13. Draw a picture of Experiment 2. Label the variables.

Work with your group to develop a procedure for accurately measuring distance and recording the data. Discuss your method with your teacher before you collect your data.

14. Collect the data. Copy the following data table and fill in the information.

Experiment 2: Three-Second Race

Name	Activity	D Average Distance in ____	t Time in ____	S in ft/s Speed in Feet per Second

168   SG • Grade 5 • Unit 5 • Lesson 5   A Day at the Races

Student Guide - page 168 (Answers on p. 95)

The Three-Second Race is similar to the Sack Race described in the *Student Guide* except that each participant in this race chooses a different way to move. Each person moves for three seconds and students measure the distance traveled. Students should work with the same groups as in Experiment 1 and group members should choose from the same activities. However, each member should choose a different activity from the one they chose in Experiment 1. This will make the data analysis more interesting.

Groups should develop a procedure for accurately measuring the distance traveled in three seconds. One way to set up the experiment is to draw a starting line and a track. One student should stand at the starting line, another with a piece of chalk should stand along the track, and a third should use a

stopwatch. Each participant should begin traveling behind the starting line and when his or her foot crosses the starting line, the person posted there says, "Go." The timer starts the watch and after three seconds says, "Now." At that signal, the student with the chalk marks the location of the participant's front foot. The distance between the starting line and the chalk mark is measured in feet and recorded. Since many errors in measurement are possible, it is a good idea to take more than one trial for each student. Repeat trials that result in data that is not reasonable. Students draw pictures of their setups *(Question 13)*. Sample data are shown in Figure 27.

The data from the table in Figure 27 are transferred to a *Five-column Data Table* as in Figure 28 and graphed as in Figure 29 *(Questions 14–15)*.

Experiment 2: Three-Second Race

Name and Activity	D Distance in Feet			
	Trial 1	Trial 2	Trial 3	Median
John Crawling	6	5	8	6
Nila Running	30	33	28	30
Jessie Walking	19	17	18	18
Arti Walking Backward	15	14	17	15

Figure 27: *Organizing the data from three trials and recording the average distance*

Experiment 2: Three-Second Race

Name	Activity	D Average Distance in feet	t Time in seconds	S in ft/s Speed in Feet per Second
John	Crawling	6	3	6 ft/3 s
Nila	Running	30	3	30 ft/3 s
Jessie	Walking	18	3	18 ft/3 s
Arti	Walking Backward	15	3	15 ft/3 s

Figure 28: *Recording speeds for each member of the group as a fraction*

Experiment 2: Three-Second Race

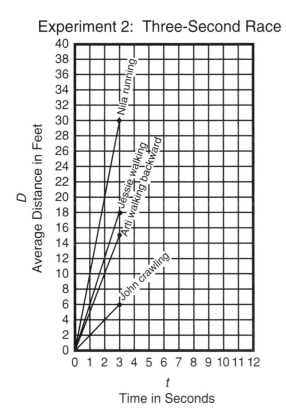

Figure 29: *Sample graph for Experiment 2: Three-Second Race*

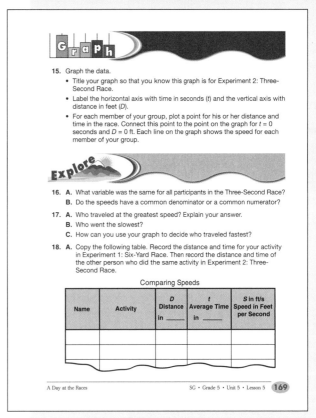

Student Guide - page 169 *(Answers on p. 95)*

TIMS Tip

As students begin the questions in the Explore section of the *A Day at the Races* Lab Pages in the *Student Guide,* you might want to announce that you will examine their work using the *Telling Rubric.* Students can use the rubric as a guide for answering the questions.

Question 17 asks who traveled the fastest in the Three-Second Race. Since the time (the denominator) was held fixed in this experiment, the distances in the numerators can be compared: the greater the distance the greater the speed. Using the graph, students see that the steepest line shows the greatest speed.

Question 18 asks students to compare the speed for an activity in Experiment 1 to the speed for the same activity in Experiment 2. For example, John's speed running in the Six-Yard Race can be compared to Nila's speed running in the Three-Second Race. Using the sample data for both experiments, Figure 30 shows a sample data table.

Comparing Speeds

Name	Activity	D Distance in *feet*	t Average Time in *seconds*	S in ft/s Speed in Feet per Second
John	Running	18	2.33	18 ft/2.33 s
Nila	Running	30	3	30 ft/3 s

Figure 30: *Comparing speeds as fractions with unlike denominators and numerators*

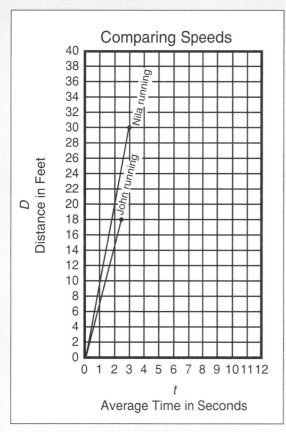

Comparing Speeds

Figure 31: *Using a graph to compare speeds*

B. Plot the data points in the table for each person, and connect each point to the point for $t = 0$ seconds and $D = 0$ feet.

C. Who went faster? How do you know?

19. Use your data and graph from Experiment 1: Six-Yard Race to answer the following:

A. How long did it take you to go 9 feet?

B. If you could travel at the same speed for 36 feet, how long would it take?

20. Use your data and graph from Experiment 2: Three-Second Race to answer the following:

A. How far did you travel in 1.5 seconds?

B. How far would you have gone in 6 seconds at the same speed?

◆Homework◆

1. Jessie traveled 22 ft in the Three-Second Race, and David traveled 25 ft in the Three-Second Race. Who traveled at the greater speed?

2. Irma ran and Nicholas jumped in the Six-Yard Race. Irma's speed was $\frac{6 \text{ yds}}{2.3 \text{ s}}$, and Nicholas's speed was $\frac{6 \text{ yds}}{3 \text{ s}}$. Who traveled faster?

3. If Manny ran 2 meters and Michael ran 4 meters, could you tell who was traveling faster? Explain.

4. If Lee Yah traveled for 4 hours and Blanca traveled for 3 hours, could you tell who was traveling faster? Explain.

5. Shannon runs 9 meters in 5 seconds. Felicia runs 6 meters in 4 seconds. Who traveled at the faster speed? Show how you know. (*Hint:* Write each speed as a ratio written as a fraction. Then compare fractions.)

6. A car moves at a constant speed of 20 meters per second. How far will it travel in 5 seconds?

7. Lin can ride 2 blocks in 5 minutes on her bicycle. How long will it take her to ride 6 blocks if she travels at the same speed?

8. Romesh walked 2 miles in a half-hour. Nila walked 4 miles in 40 minutes. Who walked faster? Show how you know.

 SG • Grade 5 • Unit 5 • Lesson 5   A Day at the Races

Student Guide - page 170 (Answers on p. 96)

Since there is no common numerator or denominator, students must choose a different strategy to compare the ratios. One solution is to graph the data as in Figure 31. The steeper line represents the greater speed. The graph tells us that Nila ran faster.

In *Questions 19–20* students use the data to make predictions. To answer *Question 19A,* students can use their graphs from Experiment 1 to estimate how long it took them to travel 9 feet. For example, using the sample data in Figure 26, Nila took a little more than 5 seconds to crawl 9 feet while John only took a little more than 1 second to run 9 feet. To answer *Question 19B,* students will need another strategy if the point for 36 feet is not on the graph. For example, they can reason that since John took 2.33 seconds to run 18 feet, he would take twice as long or 4.66 seconds to run 36 feet.

Math Facts

DPP items K and O use fact families to review the multiplication and division facts for the 9s.

Homework and Practice

- Assign the Homework section in the *Student Guide* at the end of the lab.

- Assign some or all of the word problems in Lesson 8.

- Assign DPP items L–N. Item L reviews the area model for fractions. Items M and N review computation and estimation.

- Assign Part 3 of the Home Practice which uses a graph to explore ratios.

Answers for Part 3 of the Home Practice are in the Answer Key at the end of this lesson and at the end of this unit.

Assessment

- To determine grades for this lab, assign points to one or more of the lab sections. You might choose to examine how students create data tables to organize their information. Observe students as they create the data tables in this activity. Make sure they appropriately label the column heads, their units, and title each table. See the Assessment section in the *Teacher Implementation Guide* for more suggestions for grading labs.

- Use *Question 18* to assess students' abilities to draw a graph and use it to solve problems. In this case, they can use the graph to compare speeds. You may want to use the *Telling* Rubric to score students' work on this problem.

- Use *Questions 19–20* to assess students' abilities to solve a problem and communicate their solutions. Encourage them to use the Student Rubric: *Telling* as they write their solutions. Then, using the rubric as a guide, make comments, and give students an opportunity to revise their work. You can score their responses using the *TIMS Multidimensional Rubric* in the Assessment section of the *Teacher Implementation Guide.*

- Include students' completed labs in their collection folders.

- Use the *Observational Assessment Record* and the Assessment Indicators to record and evaluate students' skills in measuring length.

Extension

DPP item P provides a challenging problem using ratios in the context of speed.

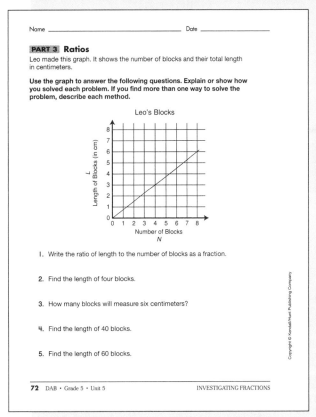

Name _____ Date _____

PART 3 **Ratios**

Leo made this graph. It shows the number of blocks and their total length in centimeters.

Use the graph to answer the following questions. Explain or show how you solved each problem. If you find more than one way to solve the problem, describe each method.

Leo's Blocks

1. Write the ratio of length to the number of blocks as a fraction.

2. Find the length of four blocks.

3. How many blocks will measure six centimeters?

4. Find the length of 40 blocks.

5. Find the length of 60 blocks.

INVESTIGATING FRACTIONS

***Discovery Assignment Book* - page 72 (*Answers on p. 96*)**

At a Glance

Math Facts and Daily Practice and Problems

Complete DPP items K–P. Items K and O review math facts. Item L reviews fractions. Items M and N provide practice with computation. Item P is a problem involving ratios and speed.

Part 1. Speed and Velocity

Students read and discuss *Questions 1–4* on *A Day at the Races* Lab Pages in the *Student Guide.*

Part 2. Experiment 1: Six-Yard Race

1. Students follow the directions in the *Student Guide* and set up Experiment 1. They lay out a 6-yard track. Students draw pictures of the experimental setup. *(Question 5)*
2. Students time each other with stopwatches as they travel down the six-yard track. They organize and record their data. *(Question 6)*
3. Students graph the data. *(Questions 7–8)*
4. Students answer questions about Experiment 1 in the Explore section of the *Student Guide.* *(Questions 9–12)*

Part 3. Experiment 2: Three-Second Race

1. Students follow the directions in the *Student Guide* and set up Experiment 2. They draw a picture of the lab setup. *(Question 13)*
2. Students time each other with a stopwatch as they travel down a track. They measure the distance each person travels after three seconds. They organize and record their data. *(Question 14)*
3. Students graph their data. *(Question 15)*
4. Students answer questions about Experiment 2 in the Explore section of the *Student Guide.* *(Questions 16–20)*

Homework

1. Assign the Homework section in the *Student Guide.*
2. Assign the word problems in Lesson 8 for homework.
3. Assign Part 3 of the Home Practice.

Assessment

1. Assign points to one or more sections of the lab to determine a grade.
2. Use *Question 18* to assess students' abilities to draw a graph. Use *Questions 19–20* to assess the students' abilities to solve problems and communicate solutions.
3. Use the *Observational Assessment Record* and the Assessment Indicators to record students' skills in measuring length.

Extension

Assign DPP item P.

Answer Key is on pages 93–96.

Notes:

Name _____   Date _____

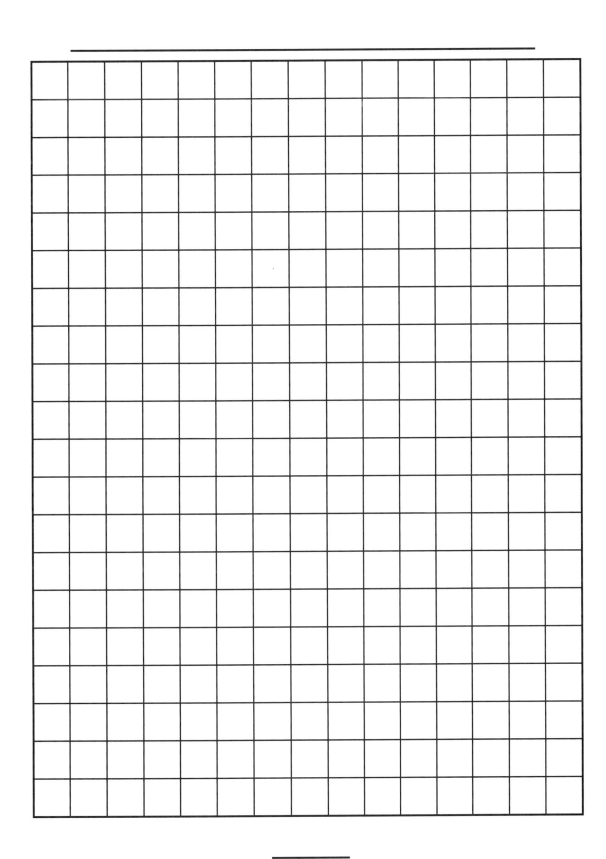

Name _____   Date _____

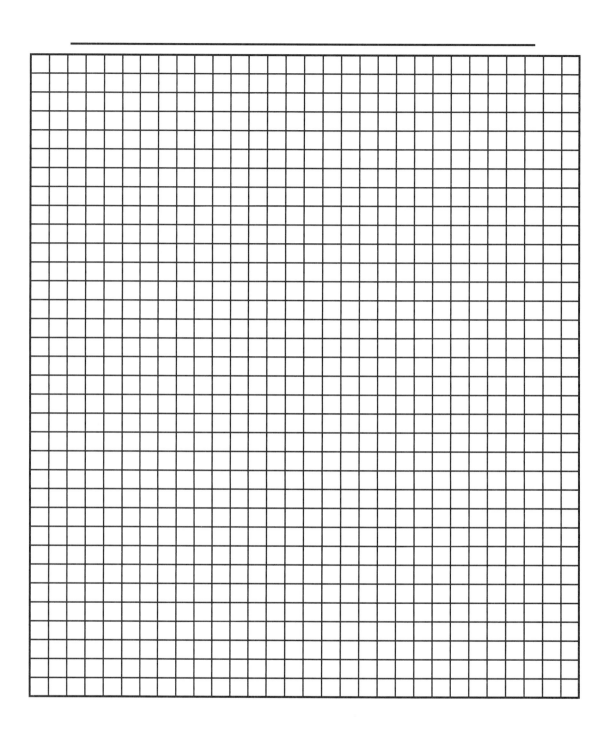

Name _____   Date _____

_____

		Trial 1	Trial 2	Trial 3	Average

Three-trial Data Table, Blackline Master

Name _____ Date _____

Five-column Data Table, Blackline Master

Student Guide (p. 164)

1.* **A.** Edward. He traveled a greater distance in 3 seconds.

   B. time, distance, and speed

   C. time and distance

   D. time

2.* **A.** Jackie. She traveled the 6 yards in less time.

   B. time, distance, and speed

   C. time and distance

   D. distance

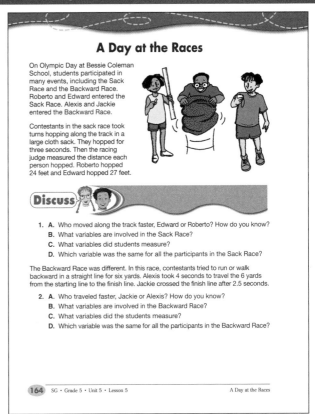

Student Guide - page 164

Student Guide (p. 165)

3. **A.** distance

   B. time

4. both time and distance

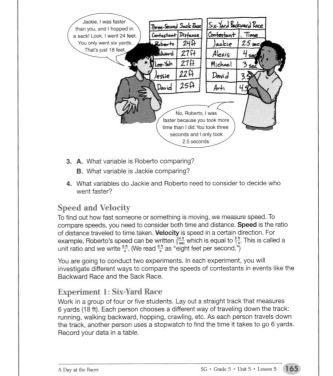

Student Guide - page 165

*Answers and/or discussion are included in the Lesson Guide.

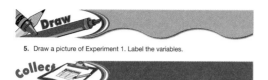

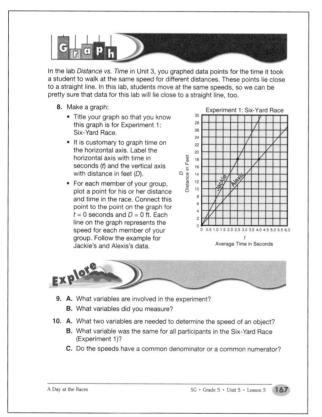

Student Guide - page 166

Student Guide (p. 166)

5. See Figure 23 in Lesson Guide 5 for a sample picture.*

6. See Figures 24–25 in Lesson Guide 5 for sample data tables.*

7. 0 s *(t)* and 0 ft *(D)**

Student Guide - page 167

Student Guide (p. 167)

8. See Figure 26 in Lesson Guide 5 for a sample graph.*

9.* **A.** time, distance, speed, and the activity chosen by each student

   B. time and distance

10. **A.** time and distance*

   B. distance

   C. numerator

*Answers and/or discussion are included in the Lesson Guide.

Student Guide (p. 168)

11.*A. Using sample data in Figures 25–26, John.

B. Using sample data in Figures 25–26, Nila.

12.*A. Using the data table, students can compare fractions since the numerators are the same. The ratio with the smallest denominator is the fastest speed.

B. Using the graph, the steeper the line, the greater the speed.

13. Answers will vary. The pictures will be similar to pictures drawn for Experiment 1 as in Figure 23 in Lesson Guide 5, but the distance is not fixed at 6 yards.

14. See Figures 27–28 in Lesson Guide 5 for sample data tables.*

11. **A.** Who traveled at the greatest speed?
    B. Who went the slowest?

12. **A.** Explain how to use the data table to compare speeds.
    B. Explain how to use the graph to compare speeds.

Experiment 2: Three-Second Race
Work with the same group of students. Use the same activities as before, but each person should choose a different way of moving. (For example, if you crawled in the Six-Yard Race, you should not crawl in the Three-Second Race.) For this experiment, each person travels for 3 seconds. Another member of the group measures the distance traveled in feet.

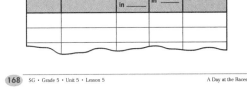

13. Draw a picture of Experiment 2. Label the variables.

Work with your group to develop a procedure for accurately measuring distance and recording the data. Discuss your method with your teacher before you collect your data.

14. Collect the data. Copy the following data table and fill in the information.

Experiment 2: Three-Second Race

Name	Activity	D Average Distance in ____	t Time in ____	S in ft/s Speed in Feet per Second

Student Guide - page 168

Student Guide (p. 169)

15. See Figure 29 in Lesson Guide 5 for a sample graph.*

16. A. time

B. common denominator

17.*A. Using sample data in Figures 28–29, Nila.

B. Using sample data in Figures 28–29, John.

C. The speed shown by the steepest line is the greatest speed.

18.*A. See Figure 30 in Lesson Guide 5 for a sample data table.

B. See Figure 31 in Lesson Guide 5 for a sample graph.

C. Using the sample data in Figures 30–31, Nila ran faster. The line on the graph for Nila's run is the steepest.

15. Graph the data.
    • Title your graph so that you know this graph is for Experiment 2: Three-Second Race.
    • Label the horizontal axis with time in seconds (t) and the vertical axis with distance in feet (D).
    • For each member of your group, plot a point for his or her distance and time in the race. Connect this point to the point on the graph for t = 0 seconds and D = 0 ft. Each line on the graph shows the speed for each member of your group.

16. **A.** What variable was the same for all participants in the Three-Second Race?
    B. Do the speeds have a common denominator or a common numerator?

17. **A.** Who traveled at the greatest speed? Explain your answer.
    B. Who went the slowest?
    C. How can you use your graph to decide who traveled fastest?

18. **A.** Copy the following table. Record the distance and time for your activity in Experiment 1: Six-Yard Race. Then record the distance and time of the other person who did the same activity in Experiment 2: Three-Second Race.

Comparing Speeds

Name	Activity	D Distance in ____	t Average Time in ____	S in ft/s Speed in Feet per Second

Student Guide - page 169

*Answers and/or discussion are included in the Lesson Guide.

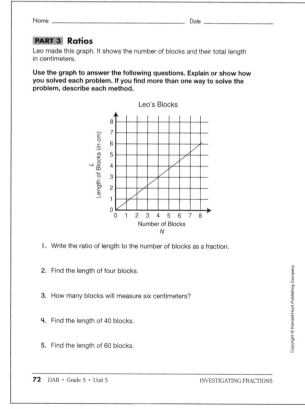

B. Plot the data points in the table for each person, and connect each point to the point for $t = 0$ seconds and $D = 0$ feet.

C. Who went faster? How do you know?

19. Use your data and graph from Experiment 1: Six-Yard Race to answer the following:

A. How long did it take you to go 9 feet?

B. If you could travel at the same speed for 36 feet, how long would it take?

20. Use your data and graph from Experiment 2: Three-Second Race to answer the following:

A. How far did you travel in 1.5 seconds?

B. How far would you have gone in 6 seconds at the same speed?

 Homework

1. Jessie traveled 22 ft in the Three-Second Race, and David traveled 25 ft in the Three-Second Race. Who traveled at the greater speed?

2. Irma ran and Nicholas jumped in the Six-Yard Race. Irma's speed was $\frac{6 \text{ yds}}{2.3 \text{ s}}$, and Nicholas's speed was $\frac{6 \text{ yds}}{3 \text{ s}}$. Who traveled faster?

3. If Manny ran 2 meters and Michael ran 4 meters, could you tell who was traveling faster? Explain.

4. If Lee Yah traveled for 4 hours and Blanca traveled for 3 hours, could you tell who was traveling faster? Explain.

5. Shannon runs 9 meters in 5 seconds. Felicia runs 6 meters in 4 seconds. Who traveled at the faster speed? Show how you know. (*Hint:* Write each speed as a ratio written as a fraction. Then compare fractions.)

6. A car moves at a constant speed of 20 meters per second. How far will it travel in 5 seconds?

7. Lin can ride 2 blocks in 5 minutes on her bicycle. How long will it take her to ride 6 blocks if she travels at the same speed?

8. Romesh walked 2 miles in a half-hour. Nila walked 4 miles in 40 minutes. Who walked faster? Show how you know.

170   SG • Grade 5 • Unit 5 • Lesson 5   A Day at the Races

Student Guide - page 170

Name _____ Date _____

PART 3 Ratios

Leo made this graph. It shows the number of blocks and their total length in centimeters.

Use the graph to answer the following questions. Explain or show how you solved each problem. If you find more than one way to solve the problem, describe each method.

Leo's Blocks

[graph: Length of Blocks (in cm) L vs. Number of Blocks N]

1. Write the ratio of length to the number of blocks as a fraction.

2. Find the length of four blocks.

3. How many blocks will measure six centimeters?

4. Find the length of 40 blocks.

5. Find the length of 60 blocks.

72   DAB • Grade 5 • Unit 5   INVESTIGATING FRACTIONS

Discovery Assignment Book - page 72

Student Guide (p. 170)

19.–20. Answers will vary.*

Homework

1. David

2. Irma

3. No, you need to know how far they traveled in a certain amount of time.

4. No, you need to know how far they traveled in a certain amount of time.

5. Shannon. At the same rates, Shannon travels 36 meters in 20 seconds while Felicia travels 30 meters in 20 seconds.

6. 100 meters

7. 15 minutes

8. Nila. Romesh walks 2 miles in 30 minutes while Nila walks 2 miles in 20 minutes. Other strategies are possible.

Discovery Assignment Book (p. 72)

Home Practice†

Part 3. Ratios

Solution strategies will vary for *Questions 1–5.*

1. Ratios will vary. One possible ratio is $\frac{3 \text{ cm}}{4 \text{ blocks}}$.

2. 3 cm

3. 8 blocks

4. 30 cm

5. 45 cm

*Answers and/or discussion are included in the Lesson Guide.
†Answers for all the Home Practice in the *Discoveery Assignment Book* are at the end of the unit.

Lesson 6

Adding Fractions with Rectangles

Estimated Class Sessions

2

Students estimate the answers to addition problems with fractions. They add fractions using common denominators by modeling rectangles on dot paper.

Key Content

- Estimating sums using benchmarks of 0, $\frac{1}{2}$, and 1.
- Finding a common denominator for fractions using pictures.
- Adding fractions with unlike denominators using pictures.

Key Vocabulary

- common denominator

Math Facts

Complete DPP item S, which is a quiz on the facts.

Homework

1. You may assign *Questions 15–25* in the Explore section for homework.
2. Assign homework *Questions 1–10* in the *Student Guide*.

Assessment

1. Use *Questions 5–6* in the Homework section to assess students' skills.
2. Use DPP Task T *Comparing Fractions* as a quiz.

Curriculum Sequence

Before This Unit

In fourth grade students added and subtracted fractions with like denominators using fraction strips in Unit 12 Lesson 2. They added fractions with unlike denominators by modeling the fractions using pattern blocks in Grade 4 Unit 12 Lessons 6 and 7.

In Grade 5 Unit 3 Lessons 2–4, students wrote addition number sentences to represent pattern block figures, developed procedures for finding equivalent fractions, and compared fractions using benchmarks of 0, $\frac{1}{2}$, and 1.

After This Unit

In fifth grade students will continue to develop meaningful procedures for adding and subtracting fractions. In Unit 11 they learn to reduce fractions to lowest terms. In Unit 12 students model addition and subtraction of fractions using pattern blocks to develop further paper-and-pencil procedures to add and subtract fractions.

Materials List

Supplies and Copies

Student	Teacher
Supplies for Each Student • crayons or markers	**Supplies**
Copies • 3–4 copies of *Centimeter Dot Paper* per student (*Unit Resource Guide* Page 36)	**Copies/Transparencies** • 1 transparency of *Centimeter Dot Paper* (*Unit Resource Guide* Page 36)

All blackline masters including assessment, transparency, and DPP masters are also on the Teacher Resource CD.

Student Books
Number Lines for Fractohoppers Chart (*Student Guide* Page 82)
Adding Fractions with Rectangles (*Student Guide* Pages 171–176)

Daily Practice and Problems and Home Practice
DPP items Q–T (*Unit Resource Guide* Pages 24–25)

Note: Classrooms whose pacing differs significantly from the suggested pacing of the units should use the Math Facts Calendar in Section 4 of the *Facts Resource Guide* to ensure students receive the complete math facts program.

Daily Practice and Problems

Suggestions for using the DPPs are on page 104.

Q. Bit: Estimating Answer Size (URG p. 24)

Without solving these problems on paper, name the number of digits in the answer.

A. $112 + 658$

B. $122 + 967$

C. $1221 - 345$

D. $3042 - 1132$

E. 5×520

S. Bit: Quiz: 9s (URG p. 24)

A. $9 \times 5 =$ B. $18 \div 2 =$

C. $27 \div 9 =$ D. $9 \times 10 =$

E. $8 \times 9 =$ F. $4 \times 9 =$

G. $81 \div 9 =$ H. $7 \times 9 =$

I. $54 \div 6 =$

R. Task: Estimating Sums (URG p. 24)

Estimate each sum using the benchmarks 0, $\frac{1}{2}$, and 1 to help you. You may use the Number Lines for Fractohoppers chart in the *Student Guide* in Unit 3 Lesson 4.

A. $\frac{4}{5} + \frac{7}{8} =$ B. $\frac{3}{9} - \frac{3}{8} =$

C. $\frac{1}{12} + \frac{3}{7} + \frac{5}{8} =$ D. $\frac{7}{11} - \frac{2}{9} =$

E. $\frac{4}{5} - \frac{3}{8} =$ F. $\frac{1}{12} + \frac{5}{10} =$

T. Task: Comparing Fractions
(URG p. 25)

Write a number sentence to compare the following fractions. Use $<$, $>$, or $=$ in your sentence. Explain your thinking for Questions A and B. Be prepared to share your strategies for the others.

A. $\frac{1}{10}, \frac{7}{8}$ B. $\frac{4}{8}, \frac{5}{10}$ C. $\frac{4}{5}, \frac{1}{2}$

D. $\frac{2}{3}, \frac{7}{12}$ E. $\frac{3}{10}, \frac{3}{8}$ F. $\frac{11}{12}, \frac{5}{12}$

In Part 1 students use benchmark fractions of 0, $\frac{1}{2}$, and 1 to estimate answers to addition problems with fractions. In Part 2 they apply previously learned fraction concepts and skills to the problem of adding fractions. This lesson develops students' number sense with fractions and gives them a conceptual basis for adding fractions. Students compute using rectangles on dot paper, connect their drawings with symbols, and check the reasonableness of their answers. They are not expected to add using only symbols or to give their answers in lowest terms. They will begin to develop paper-and-pencil procedures in Lesson 7 and continue the development in Units 11 and 12.

Part 1 Estimating Sums

The Estimating Sums section of the *Adding Fractions with Rectangles* Activity Pages in the *Student Guide* begins with a short review of using benchmarks (0, $\frac{1}{2}$, 1) to compare fractions. *Questions 3–4* ask students to use the benchmarks to estimate sums. For example, to estimate $\frac{7}{8} + \frac{5}{6}$, students can say that since both $\frac{7}{8}$ and $\frac{5}{6}$ are close to 1, the sum of the two fractions is close to 2 *(Question 3A).* As students make their estimates, encourage them to think about fraction models they used this year. For example, they can form a mental picture of pattern blocks to estimate the sum of $\frac{11}{12}$ and $\frac{1}{2}$.

Questions 5–6 deal with estimating sums involving fourths. Since $\frac{1}{4}$ is exactly midway between 0 and $\frac{1}{2}$, we do not want to group $\frac{1}{4}$ with the fractions near 0 nor with the fractions near $\frac{1}{2}$. Students will need to develop strategies for estimating sums with $\frac{1}{4}$ and $\frac{3}{4}$. For example, *Question 6B* asks students to estimate the sum of $\frac{3}{4} + \frac{1}{10}$. Since $\frac{3}{4}$ is midway between $\frac{1}{2}$ and 1 and since $\frac{1}{10}$ is just a little greater than 0, the sum is less than one. *Questions 7–8* deal in a similar way with estimating sums involving thirds. Using the Number Lines for Fractohoppers chart in the *Student Guide* in Unit 3 Lesson 4 may help students visualize the relative size of the fractions. A class discussion of estimation strategies will enhance individual students' number sense and estimation skills.

Part 2 Adding Fractions with Rectangles on Dot Paper

Questions 9–14 in the Adding Fractions with Rectangles on Dot Paper section of the *Student Guide* explore dividing rectangles into parts to model an addition problem, estimating the sum, and choosing the right size rectangle to model one whole. Estimating the sum helps students decide whether to use one or two rectangles to model the addition. For example, since $\frac{3}{4} + \frac{4}{5}$ is greater than one, they need two rectangles to model the sum. Choosing the appropriate

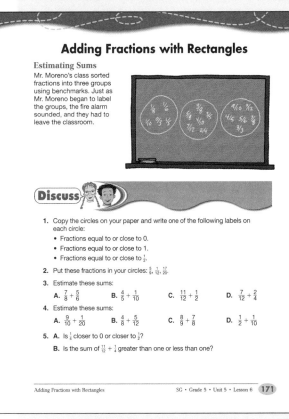

Student Guide - page 171 *(Answers on p. 106)*

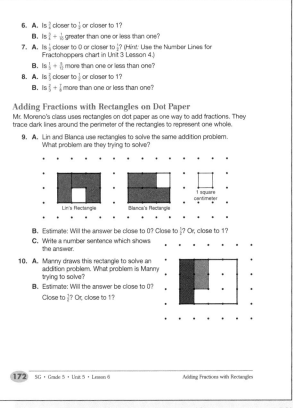

Student Guide - page 172 *(Answers on p. 106)*

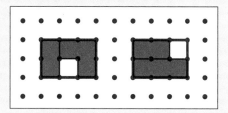

Figure 32: *Two ways to model*
$\frac{1}{3} + \frac{1}{2} = \frac{5}{6}$

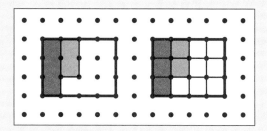

Figure 33: $\frac{1}{4} + \frac{1}{6} = \frac{3}{12} + \frac{2}{12} = \frac{5}{12}$

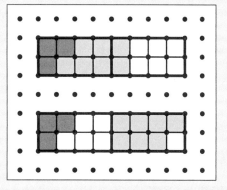

Figure 34: *Two ways to model* $\frac{3}{8} + \frac{7}{8}$

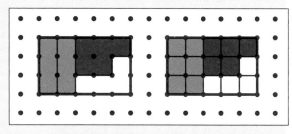

Figure 35: $\frac{2}{5} + \frac{1}{3} = \frac{6}{15} + \frac{5}{15} = \frac{11}{15}$

rectangle for one whole models choosing a common denominator. Since a rectangle with an area of 20 sq cm can be divided into fourths and fifths, you can use a 4 × 5 rectangle to represent one whole.

Question 9 shows two ways to model the same addition problem. Students must identify the problem, estimate the result, and write a number sentence that gives the answer. See Figure 32.

To help students with ***Question 9,*** ask

- *What fraction is shown in blue in both rectangles?* ($\frac{1}{3}$. If a student says this fraction is $\frac{2}{6}$, point out that $\frac{2}{6} = \frac{1}{3}$. We are interested in the problem $\frac{1}{3} + \frac{1}{2}$.)

- *What fraction is shown in red in both rectangles?* ($\frac{1}{2}$)

- *What is the area of the whole rectangle?* (6 sq cm)

- *How many square centimeters are colored?* (5 sq cm)

- *What fraction of the whole rectangle is colored in?* ($\frac{5}{6}$)

- *Give a number sentence for this problem.* ($\frac{1}{3} + \frac{1}{2} = \frac{5}{6}$ or $\frac{2}{6} + \frac{3}{6} = \frac{5}{6}$)

Question 10 uses a rectangle to model the addition problem $\frac{1}{4} + \frac{1}{6}$. In ***Question 11*** a second rectangle models rewriting the problem with a common denominator: $\frac{3}{12} + \frac{2}{12} = \frac{5}{12}$. See Figure 33.

Question 12 models the sum of $\frac{3}{8} + \frac{7}{8}$. Since the sum is greater than one, two rectangles joined together are used to solve the problem. Students can choose to shade the fractions in more than one way. For example, Figure 34 shows two ways to model $\frac{3}{8} + \frac{7}{8}$.

Students must finish a problem in ***Question 13.*** Students are asked to model the problem $\frac{2}{5} + \frac{1}{3}$. They are shown a 3 × 5 rectangle with $\frac{2}{5}$ shaded. They must decide how to shade $\frac{1}{3}$ in the unshaded portion of the rectangle. Students are then asked to change their rectangle to show fifteenths. One possible model is shown in Figure 35.

If students need help with ***Question 13,*** ask

- *How many square centimeters are in the whole rectangle?* (15 sq cm)

- *How many square centimeters are in $\frac{1}{3}$ of the rectangle?* (5 sq cm. If necessary, students can sketch a 3 × 5 rectangle, shade $\frac{1}{3}$, and count square centimeters to find $\frac{1}{3}$ of 15 sq cm. Then they can find a way to shade 5 sq cm on the rectangle in the unshaded portion of the rectangle.)

Question 14 asks students to choose the appropriate rectangle to model one whole. To model $\frac{2}{3} + \frac{1}{4}$, they can use a 3 × 4 rectangle since a rectangle with an area of 12 sq cm can be divided into both thirds and fourths.

Questions 15–21 provide practice adding fractions with rectangles. Note that we do not ask for the least common denominator. Any common denominator will do. For example, to model $\frac{1}{4} + \frac{7}{10}$ **(Question 18),** students can use a 20 sq cm rectangle or a 40 sq cm rectangle, so both answers $\frac{19}{20}$ and $\frac{38}{40}$ are acceptable. When they complete the question, ask students which rectangles they chose and why. Some may say it is easier to use a smaller rectangle since they do not have to draw as much, while others may say it is easier to fit the fractions into the larger rectangle.

Encourage students to use number sense and reasoning to complete **Questions 22–25.** For example, for **Question 22** students can "skip count" by fourths. They can say, "I know $\frac{1}{2}$ equals $\frac{2}{4}$ and $\frac{1}{4}$ more is $\frac{3}{4}$." Students can also use rectangles.

Journal Prompt

You have decided to bake a cake for your family. The recipe calls for $1\frac{3}{4}$ cups of sugar. You can only find two of the measuring cups, the $\frac{1}{2}$ cup and the $\frac{1}{8}$ cup. Write a number sentence showing how you could use these two cups to measure $1\frac{3}{4}$ cups of sugar. Write about your solution. (Challenge: Can you find more than one solution to this problem?)

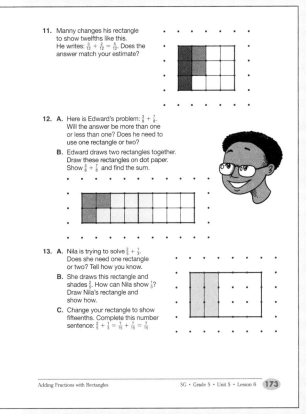

Student Guide - page 173 (Answers on p. 107)

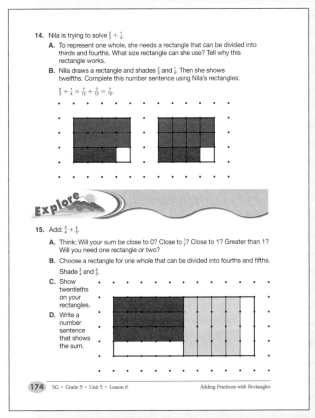

Student Guide - page 174 (Answers on p. 107)

Draw fraction rectangles to help you solve the following problems. Show all your work. Is your answer reasonable?

16. $\frac{3}{10} + \frac{9}{10} = ?$

(*Hint:* Will the sum be close to 0? Close to $\frac{1}{2}$? Close to 1? Greater than 1?)

17. $\frac{1}{4} + \frac{3}{8} = ?$ **18.** $\frac{1}{4} + \frac{7}{10} = ?$ **19.** $\frac{5}{8} + \frac{1}{4} = ?$

20. Blanca and Lin bought one sandwich at the deli. Blanca ate $\frac{1}{2}$ of the sandwich, and Lin ate $\frac{3}{8}$ of it. How much of the whole sandwich did the two girls eat?

21. Manny and Frank ordered pizza. Manny ate $\frac{1}{4}$ of the pizza, and Frank ate $\frac{5}{8}$ of the pizza. How much of the whole pizza was eaten?

Solve the following problems. Choose your own strategy. Estimate to see if your answers are reasonable.

22. $\frac{1}{2} + \frac{1}{4}$ **23.** $\frac{1}{2} + \frac{3}{4}$ **24.** $\frac{1}{12} + \frac{7}{12}$ **25.** $\frac{1}{2} + \frac{5}{10}$

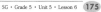 **Homework**

1. Give **estimates** for these sums.

A. $\frac{7}{8} + \frac{9}{10}$ B. $\frac{2}{5} + \frac{1}{12}$ C. $\frac{3}{5} + \frac{5}{12}$

Use rectangles on dot paper to solve the following problems. For each problem:

- Estimate the answer.
- Choose a rectangle for one whole.
- Decide if you will need one rectangle or two to solve the problem.
- Show your work. Write a number sentence for your solution.
- Look back and check if your answer is reasonable.

2. $\frac{5}{12} + \frac{2}{3}$ **3.** $\frac{2}{3} + \frac{1}{6}$ **4.** $\frac{7}{10} + \frac{1}{2}$ **5.** $\frac{3}{4} + \frac{1}{3}$

Student Guide - page 175 *(Answers on p. 108)*

Solve Questions 6–10. Explain your solutions.

6. After school, Blanca walked $\frac{1}{2}$ mile to the park. She then walked another block, or $\frac{1}{8}$ of a mile, farther to the store. How far did Blanca walk?

7. Shannon and Jackie shared an apple. Shannon ate $\frac{1}{4}$ of the apple. Jackie ate $\frac{1}{3}$ of the apple. How much of the apple was left?

8. Jessie's mom baked an apple pie for dessert. The family ate $\frac{3}{8}$ of the pie the first night. They ate $\frac{1}{4}$ of the pie the next night. How much of the pie was eaten?

9. Jessie's mom used $\frac{1}{2}$ cup of white sugar and $\frac{1}{3}$ cup of brown sugar. How many cups did she use altogether?

10. Shannon ran $\frac{5}{8}$ of a mile. Then she walked $\frac{3}{4}$ mile. Did she go more or less than 1 mile? How do you know?

Student Guide - page 176 *(Answers on p. 109)*

Math Facts

DPP item S quizzes students on the multiplication and division facts for the 9s.

Homework and Practice

- Assign *Questions 15–25* in the Explore section.
- Assign homework *Questions 1–10* in the *Student Guide*.
- Assign DPP item R to review fraction concepts. Item Q provides practice estimating with whole numbers.

Assessment

- Use *Questions 5–6* in the Homework section to check students' skills at solving addition problems.
- Use DPP Task T to quiz students on comparing fractions.

At a Glance

Math Facts and Daily Practice and Problems

Complete DPP items Q–T. Item S is a quiz on the facts. Items R and T practice fraction concepts. Item Q involves computation and estimation.

Part 1. Estimating Sums

1. Review using benchmarks of 0, $\frac{1}{2}$, and 1 to compare fractions. *(Questions 1–2)*
2. Use benchmarks to estimate the sum of two fractions. *(Questions 3–4)*
3. Discuss estimating sums of fractions with thirds and fourths. *(Questions 5–8)*

Part 2. Adding Fractions with Rectangles on Dot Paper

1. Use *Questions 9–14* and the discussion prompts in the Lesson Guide to explore the use of rectangles on dot paper to add fractions.
2. Students solve *Questions 15–25* in the Explore section.

Homework

1. You may assign *Questions 15–25* in the Explore section for homework.
2. Assign homework *Questions 1–10* in the *Student Guide.*

Assessment

1. Use *Questions 5–6* in the Homework section to assess students' skills.
2. Use DPP Task T *Comparing Fractions* as a quiz.

Answer Key is on pages 106–109.

Notes:

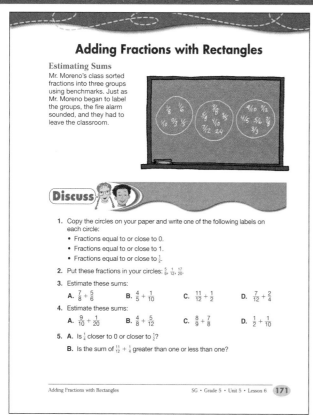

Student Guide - page 171

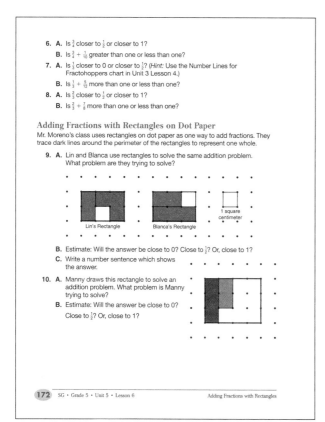

Student Guide - page 172

Student Guide (p. 171)

1.–2.

| Fractions equal to or close to 0. | Fractions equal to or close to $\frac{1}{2}$. | Fractions equal to or close to 1. |

3. A. about 2*

   B. about 1

   C. about $1\frac{1}{2}$

   D. about 1

4. A. about 1

   B. about 1

   C. about 2

   D. about $\frac{1}{2}$

5. A. It is exactly halfway between.

   B. greater than one

Student Guide (p. 172)

6. A. It is exactly halfway between.*

   B. less than one

7. A. closer to $\frac{1}{2}$

   B. less than one

8. A. closer to $\frac{1}{2}$

   B. more than one

9. A. $\frac{1}{3} + \frac{1}{2}$*

   B. close to 1

   C. $\frac{1}{3} + \frac{1}{2} = \frac{5}{6}$

10. A. $\frac{1}{4} + \frac{1}{6}$

   B. close to $\frac{1}{2}$

*Answers and/or discussion are included in the Lesson Guide.

Student Guide (p. 173)

11. yes

12. **A.** more than one, two rectangles

   B. $\frac{3}{8} + \frac{7}{8} = \frac{10}{8}$

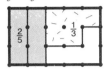

13. **A.** One rectangle; $\frac{2}{5}$ and $\frac{1}{3}$ are both close to $\frac{1}{2}$ but they are each a little less than $\frac{1}{2}$, so $\frac{2}{5} + \frac{1}{3}$ is less than one.*

   B. $\frac{2}{5} + \frac{1}{3}$

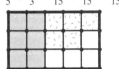

   C. $\frac{2}{5} + \frac{1}{3} = \frac{6}{15} + \frac{5}{15} = \frac{11}{15}$

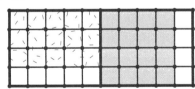

Student Guide (p. 174)

14. **A.** Answers will vary. One possibility is a 3×4 rectangle because both 3 and 4 divide evenly into 12.

   B. $\frac{2}{3} + \frac{1}{4} = \frac{8}{12} + \frac{3}{12} = \frac{11}{12}$

15. **A.** greater than one, two rectangles

   B.–C.

   D. $\frac{3}{4} + \frac{4}{5} = \frac{15}{20} + \frac{16}{20} = \frac{31}{20}$ or $1\frac{11}{20}$

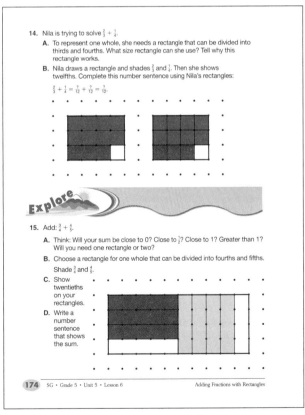

Student Guide - page 173

Student Guide - page 174

*Answers and/or discussion are included in the Lesson Guide.

Draw fraction rectangles to help you solve the following problems. Show all your work. Is your answer reasonable?

16. $\frac{3}{10} + \frac{9}{10} = ?$

(*Hint:* Will the sum be close to 0? Close to $\frac{1}{2}$? Close to 1? Greater than 1?)

17. $\frac{1}{4} + \frac{3}{8} = ?$ **18.** $\frac{1}{4} + \frac{7}{10} = ?$ **19.** $\frac{5}{6} + \frac{1}{4} = ?$

20. Blanca and Lin bought one sandwich at the deli. Blanca ate $\frac{1}{2}$ of the sandwich, and Lin ate $\frac{3}{8}$ of it. How much of the whole sandwich did the two girls eat?

21. Manny and Frank ordered pizza. Manny ate $\frac{1}{4}$ of the pizza, and Frank ate $\frac{5}{8}$ of the pizza. How much of the whole pizza was eaten?

Solve the following problems. Choose your own strategy. Estimate to see if your answers are reasonable.

22. $\frac{1}{2} + \frac{1}{4}$ **23.** $\frac{1}{2} + \frac{3}{4}$ **24.** $\frac{1}{12} + \frac{7}{12}$ **25.** $\frac{1}{2} + \frac{5}{10}$

1. Give **estimates** for these sums.

   A. $\frac{7}{8} + \frac{9}{10}$ **B.** $\frac{2}{5} + \frac{1}{12}$ **C.** $\frac{3}{5} + \frac{5}{12}$

Use rectangles on dot paper to solve the following problems. For each problem:

• Estimate the answer.
• Choose a rectangle for one whole.
• Decide if you will need one rectangle or two to solve the problem.
• Show your work. Write a number sentence for your solution.
• Look back and check if your answer is reasonable.

2. $\frac{5}{12} + \frac{2}{3}$ **3.** $\frac{2}{3} + \frac{1}{6}$ **4.** $\frac{7}{10} + \frac{1}{2}$ **5.** $\frac{3}{4} + \frac{1}{3}$

Adding Fractions with Rectangles   SG • Grade 5 • Unit 5 • Lesson 6   **175**

Student Guide - page 175

Student Guide (p. 175)

16. greater than one; $\frac{3}{10} + \frac{9}{10} = \frac{12}{10}$

17. $\frac{1}{4} + \frac{3}{8} = \frac{2}{8} + \frac{3}{8} = \frac{5}{8}$

18. $\frac{1}{4} + \frac{7}{10} = \frac{5}{20} + \frac{14}{20} = \frac{19}{20}$*

19. $\frac{5}{6} + \frac{1}{4} = \frac{10}{12} + \frac{3}{12} = \frac{13}{12}$

20. $\frac{1}{2} + \frac{3}{8} = \frac{4}{8} + \frac{3}{8} = \frac{7}{8}$

21. $\frac{1}{4} + \frac{5}{8} = \frac{2}{8} + \frac{5}{8} = \frac{7}{8}$

22. $\frac{3}{4}$*

23. $\frac{5}{4}$ or $1\frac{1}{4}$

24. $\frac{8}{12}$

25. 1

Homework

1. **A.** about 2

   B. about $\frac{1}{2}$

   C. about 1

Estimates will vary and the size of the whole will vary for *Questions 2–5.*

2. Greater than 1, a 3×4 rectangle is one whole, need two rectangles, $\frac{5}{12} + \frac{2}{3} = \frac{5}{12} + \frac{8}{12} = \frac{13}{12}$.

3. Less than 1, a 3×4 rectangle is one whole, need one rectangle, $\frac{2}{3} + \frac{1}{6} = \frac{4}{6} + \frac{1}{6} = \frac{5}{6}$.

4. Greater than 1, a 2×5 rectangle is one whole, need two rectangles, $\frac{7}{10} + \frac{1}{2} = \frac{7}{10} + \frac{5}{10} = \frac{12}{10}$.

5. About 1, a 3×4 rectangle is one whole, need two rectangles, $\frac{3}{4} + \frac{1}{3} = \frac{9}{12} + \frac{4}{12} = \frac{13}{12}$.

*Answers and/or discussion are included in the Lesson Guide.

Student Guide (p. 176)

6. $\frac{5}{8}$ of a mile. Strategies will vary.

7. $\frac{7}{12}$ of the apple was eaten; $\frac{5}{12}$ is left. Strategies will vary. One possible strategy is: $\frac{1}{4} = \frac{3}{12}$; $\frac{1}{3} = \frac{4}{12}$; $\frac{3}{12} + \frac{4}{12} = \frac{7}{12}$.

8. $\frac{5}{8}$ of a pie. Strategies will vary. One possible strategy is: $\frac{1}{4} = \frac{2}{8}$; $\frac{3}{8} + \frac{2}{8} = \frac{5}{8}$.

9. $\frac{5}{6}$ of a cup. Strategies will vary.

10. More than 1 mile. Strategies will vary.

Solve Questions 6–10. Explain your solutions.

6. After school, Blanca walked $\frac{1}{2}$ mile to the park. She then walked another block, or $\frac{1}{8}$ of a mile, farther to the store. How far did Blanca walk?

7. Shannon and Jackie shared an apple. Shannon ate $\frac{1}{4}$ of the apple. Jackie ate $\frac{1}{3}$ of the apple. How much of the apple was left?

8. Jessie's mom baked an apple pie for dessert. The family ate $\frac{3}{8}$ of the pie the first night. They ate $\frac{1}{4}$ of the pie the next night. How much of the pie was eaten?

9. Jessie's mom used $\frac{1}{2}$ cup of white sugar and $\frac{1}{3}$ cup of brown sugar. How many cups did she use altogether?

10. Shannon ran $\frac{5}{8}$ of a mile. Then she walked $\frac{3}{4}$ mile. Did she go more or less than 1 mile? How do you know?

176   SG • Grade 5 • Unit 5 • Lesson 6   Adding Fractions with Rectangles

Student Guide - page 176

Lesson 7

Adding and Subtracting Fractions

Lesson Overview

In Part 1, students subtract fractions with unlike denominators by building models using dot paper rectangles. In Part 2, students use symbols to add and subtract fractions. They find common denominators, use symbols to find equivalent fractions, and then add and subtract fractions with like denominators.

Key Content

- Estimating differences of fractions using benchmarks such as 0, $\frac{1}{2}$, and 1.
- Subtracting fractions with unlike denominators using pictures.
- Finding a common denominator for two or more fractions.
- Adding and subtracting fractions with unlike denominators using symbols.

Key Vocabulary

- common denominator

Homework

1. Assign homework *Questions 1–8* in the *Student Guide*.
2. Assign Part 6 of the Home Practice.

Assessment

Students complete the *Fraction Follow-Up* Assessment Pages.

Materials List

Supplies and Copies

Student	Teacher
Supplies for Each Student	**Supplies**
Copies • 1 copy of *Fraction Follow-Up* per student (*Unit Resource Guide* Pages 117–118) • 3–4 copies of *Centimeter Dot Paper* per student (*Unit Resource Guide* Page 36)	**Copies/Transparencies** • 1 transparency of *Centimeter Dot Paper* (*Unit Resource Guide* Page 36)

All blackline masters including assessment, transparency, and DPP masters are also on the Teacher Resource CD.

Student Books

Adding and Subtracting Fractions (*Student Guide* Pages 177–181)

Daily Practice and Problems and Home Practice

DPP items U–V (*Unit Resource Guide* Page 25)
Home Practice Part 6 (*Discovery Assignment Book* Page 74)

Note: Classrooms whose pacing differs significantly from the suggested pacing of the units should use the Math Facts Calendar in Section 4 of the *Facts Resource Guide* to ensure students receive the complete math facts program.

U. Bit: Choosing Units of Measure
   (URG p. 25)

The following are some units of measure for length: meters, centimeters, feet, inches, yards, kilometers, and miles.

Which unit of measure does it make sense to use when you measure:

1. the length of a book?
2. the distance from your classroom door to your teacher's desk?
3. the distance from your home to school?
4. a person's height?

V. Challenge: Scale Models (URG p. 25)

Frank and John both are making models of a building in their town. In John's building, 2 inches of the model represent 5 feet of the real building. In Frank's building, 5 inches represent 15 feet. Whose model will be larger? Explain why you think so.

Part 1 Subtracting Fractions

Turn to the *Adding and Subtracting Fractions* Activity Pages in the *Student Guide*. Ask students to think about **Question 1A** (estimate the difference of $\frac{2}{3} - \frac{1}{4}$). Students might reason that $\frac{2}{3} - \frac{1}{4}$ is closer to $\frac{1}{2}$ than 0 because $\frac{2}{3}$ is between $\frac{1}{2}$ and 1. Subtracting only $\frac{1}{4}$ will not bring us close to 0.

In **Questions 1B–1C,** students use dot paper rectangles to subtract $\frac{1}{4}$ from $\frac{2}{3}$. As you demonstrate this strategy on a transparency of *Centimeter Dot Paper,* have students complete the problem along with you on their own copies of dot paper. Discuss why a 3 × 4 rectangle is a good choice for this problem. (A 3 × 4 rectangle can be divided into both thirds and fourths.) First, students shade $\frac{2}{3}$ of the rectangle. Then they must determine how much to erase, that is, how many squares are $\frac{1}{4}$ of the rectangle. Encourage students to think of a clean 3 × 4 rectangle; $\frac{1}{4}$ of a 3 × 4 rectangle is one of the four columns, or 3 squares. After erasing $\frac{1}{4}$ of the rectangle or 3 squares, $\frac{5}{12}$ remains. After finding the answer, students should check back to see if it is reasonable. Are their answers close to their estimates? Looking at the answer represented on dot paper, as in Figure 36 and in the *Student Guide,* one can see that $\frac{5}{12}$ is close to the estimate of $\frac{1}{2}$.

$\frac{2}{3}$ is shaded.　$\frac{1}{4}$ is erased.　$\frac{2}{3} - \frac{1}{4} = \frac{5}{12}$

Figure 36: *Using a 3 × 4 rectangle to solve $\frac{2}{3} - \frac{1}{4}$*

To prepare for their work in Part 2, ask students to look at the dot paper rectangles in the *Student Guide* or those they created to model $\frac{2}{3} - \frac{1}{4}$. Ask them to name fractions equivalent to $\frac{2}{3}$ and $\frac{1}{4}$ with the common denominator of 12. Since $\frac{2}{3} = \frac{8}{12}$ and $\frac{1}{4} = \frac{3}{12}$, then, $\frac{8}{12} - \frac{3}{12} = \frac{5}{12}$.

In **Question 2,** students solve the problem $\frac{3}{4} - \frac{3}{8}$ using dot paper rectangles. Again, students are asked to estimate the answer before solving the problem **(Question 2A).** Students might consider $\frac{3}{4}$ as close to 1 and $\frac{3}{8}$ as close to $\frac{1}{2}$. Therefore, they might say the answer is close to $1 - \frac{1}{2}$ or $\frac{1}{2}$. Solve $\frac{3}{4} - \frac{3}{8}$ on a transparency of *Centimeter Dot Paper* using the figures in the *Student Guide* as a model. Students should solve the problem at their desks as well. A 2 × 4 rectangle is appropriate for this problem since it can be divided into fourths and eighths. By

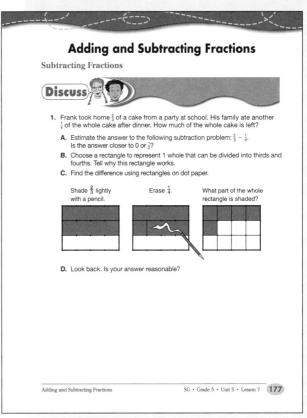

Adding and Subtracting Fractions

Subtracting Fractions

Discuss

1. Frank took home $\frac{2}{3}$ of a cake from a party at school. His family ate another $\frac{1}{4}$ of the whole cake after dinner. How much of the whole cake is left?

   A. Estimate the answer to the following subtraction problem: $\frac{2}{3} - \frac{1}{4}$. Is the answer closer to 0 or $\frac{1}{2}$?

   B. Choose a rectangle to represent 1 whole that can be divided into thirds and fourths. Tell why this rectangle works.

   C. Find the difference using rectangles on dot paper.

   Shade $\frac{2}{3}$ lightly with a pencil.　Erase $\frac{1}{4}$.　What part of the whole rectangle is shaded?

   D. Look back. Is your answer reasonable?

Student Guide - page 177 (Answers on p. 119)

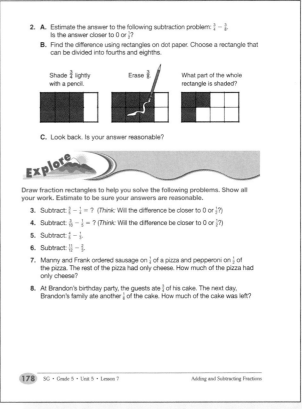

2. **A.** Estimate the answer to the following subtraction problem: $\frac{3}{4} - \frac{3}{8}$. Is the answer closer to 0 or $\frac{1}{2}$?

   B. Find the difference using rectangles on dot paper. Choose a rectangle that can be divided into fourths and eighths.

   Shade $\frac{3}{4}$ lightly with a pencil.　Erase $\frac{3}{8}$.　What part of the whole rectangle is shaded?

   C. Look back. Is your answer reasonable?

Explore

Draw fraction rectangles to help you solve the following problems. Show all your work. Estimate to be sure your answers are reasonable.

3. Subtract: $\frac{5}{8} - \frac{1}{4} = ?$ (*Think*: Will the difference be closer to 0 or $\frac{1}{2}$?)

4. Subtract: $\frac{3}{10} - \frac{1}{5} = ?$ (*Think*: Will the difference be closer to 0 or $\frac{1}{2}$?)

5. Subtract: $\frac{4}{5} - \frac{1}{3}$.

6. Subtract: $\frac{11}{12} - \frac{2}{3}$.

7. Manny and Frank ordered sausage on $\frac{1}{4}$ of a pizza and pepperoni on $\frac{1}{2}$ of the pizza. The rest of the pizza had only cheese. How much of the pizza had only cheese?

8. At Brandon's birthday party, the guests ate $\frac{3}{4}$ of his cake. The next day, Brandon's family ate another $\frac{1}{8}$ of the cake. How much of the cake was left?

Student Guide - page 178 (Answers on pp. 119–120)

Using Symbols to Add and Subtract Fractions

Discuss

You can use symbols when you add or subtract fractions.

9. A. Think about the sum of the following addition problem: $\frac{2}{3} + \frac{3}{4}$. Will it be close to one? Greater than one?

B. Twelve is a common denominator for $\frac{2}{3}$ and $\frac{3}{4}$. Why? (Think of dot paper rectangles.)

C. Using 12 as your denominator, write fractions equivalent to $\frac{2}{3}$ and $\frac{3}{4}$.

D. Then add.

$$\frac{3}{4} = \frac{?}{12} \qquad \frac{2}{3} = \frac{?}{12}$$

$$\frac{3 \times 3}{4 \times 3} = \frac{9}{12} \qquad \frac{2 \times 4}{3 \times 4} = \frac{8}{12}$$

$$\frac{3}{4} + \frac{2}{3} = \frac{9}{12} + \frac{8}{12} = \frac{17}{12}$$

E. Is the answer reasonable?

10. A. Estimate the difference for the following subtraction problem: $\frac{4}{5} - \frac{3}{4}$. Will the difference be closer to 0 or $\frac{1}{2}$?

B. Twenty is a common denominator for $\frac{4}{5}$ and $\frac{3}{4}$. Why?

C. Using 20 as your denominator, write fractions equivalent to $\frac{4}{5}$ and $\frac{3}{4}$.

D. Subtract.

$$\frac{4}{5} = \frac{?}{20} \qquad \frac{3}{4} = \frac{?}{20}$$

$$\frac{4 \times 4}{5 \times 4} = \frac{16}{20} \qquad \frac{3 \times 5}{4 \times 5} = \frac{15}{20}$$

$$\frac{4}{5} - \frac{3}{4} = \frac{16}{20} - \frac{15}{20} = \frac{1}{20}$$

E. Look back. Is the answer reasonable?

Student Guide - page 179   *(Answers on p. 120)*

---

11. A. Add: $\frac{1}{4} + \frac{3}{8}$.

B. Choose a common denominator for $\frac{1}{4}$ and $\frac{3}{8}$. Eighths will work. Why?

C. Using 8 as your denominator, write fractions equivalent to $\frac{1}{4}$ and $\frac{3}{8}$.

D. Add.

12. A. Subtract: $\frac{7}{8} - \frac{1}{2}$.

B. What is a common denominator for $\frac{7}{8}$ and $\frac{1}{2}$?

C. Using this denominator, write equivalent fractions for $\frac{7}{8}$ and $\frac{1}{2}$.

D. Subtract.

13. A. Add: $\frac{2}{3} + \frac{5}{8}$.

B. What is a common denominator for $\frac{2}{3}$ and $\frac{5}{8}$?

C. Using this denominator, write equivalent fractions for $\frac{2}{3}$ and $\frac{5}{8}$.

D. Add.

E. Look at your answer. Is there another name for this fraction?

14. A. $\frac{2}{5} + \frac{3}{10} = ?$

B. What is a common denominator for $\frac{2}{5}$ and $\frac{3}{10}$?

C. Write $\frac{2}{5}$ and $\frac{3}{10}$ with a common denominator.

D. Add.

15. $\frac{5}{6} - \frac{1}{4} = ?$ **16.** $\frac{5}{12} + \frac{3}{4} = ?$

17. $\frac{1}{5} + \frac{1}{3} = ?$ **18.** $\frac{5}{8} - \frac{1}{4} = ?$

Homework

Complete the following problems. Show your work. Estimate to be sure your answers are reasonable.

1. $\frac{4}{5} - \frac{1}{4} = ?$

2. A. $\frac{11}{12} - \frac{3}{4} = ?$

B. Look at your answer to Part A. What is another name for this fraction?

3. A. $\frac{5}{8} + \frac{1}{2} = ?$

B. Look at your answer to Part A. What is another name for this fraction?

Student Guide - page 180   *(Answers on p. 121)*

---

shading $\frac{3}{4}$ of the rectangle and erasing $\frac{3}{8}$, the answer of $\frac{3}{8}$ results, which is close to the estimate of $\frac{1}{2}$.

Questions 3–8 provide additional practice subtracting fractions, modeling the problems on dot paper. Students may work either independently or in a small group to find solutions. Discuss the strategies used. If students use rectangles of different sizes, answers will vary. For example, in ***Question 4,*** one student may answer $\frac{2}{20}$ (this student may have used a 4 × 5 rectangle) while another may answer $\frac{1}{10}$ (this student may have used a 2 × 5 rectangle). Students should realize that these two fractions are equivalent and be able to explain why.

TIMS Tip

In Unit 11 students learn to reduce fractions to lowest terms. In this lesson, students' answers should match their work with the rectangles. Therefore, many answers will not appear in lowest terms.

Part 2   **Using Symbols to Add and Subtract Fractions**

Students used symbols to find common denominators in Lesson 4. This strategy will be used in ***Questions 9–14.*** These questions lead students through a series of steps enabling them to complete addition or subtraction computations using common denominators. Begin by asking students what they need to do to add $\frac{2}{3}$ and $\frac{3}{4}$. Students should recognize they need to find a common denominator before adding these two fractions. Discuss what strategy, other than using rectangles, they can use to find a common denominator. They should suggest using symbols. Help students work through the steps in ***Question 9.*** You may want to model these steps on the overhead or board. Continue this process for ***Questions 10–11,*** also. It is important for students to understand that when you add or subtract fractions with like denominators, the denominator in the sum or difference is the same. You add or subtract the numerators.

Questions 12–18 provide additional practice. Students may answer these questions in small groups or independently. They should be able to explain the process they use to solve each problem. They may choose different common denominators, but they should be able to justify their choices. Have students compare their solutions with those of another student. If their solutions do not agree, have them determine if their answers are equivalent fractions. If the fractions are not equivalent, each student should make corrections as needed. Encourage students to use rectangles to check their work.

Journal Prompt

Nila and Jerome shared a pizza. Nila said, "I ate $\frac{3}{8}$ of the pizza."
Jerome said, "I ate $\frac{3}{4}$ of the pizza." Jessie said, "That's impossible."
Explain why Jessie is right.

Homework and Practice

- Assign homework *Questions 1–8* on the *Adding and Subtracting Fractions* Activity Pages in the *Student Guide.*

- Assign DPP item U which reviews units of measure.

- Assign Part 6 of the Home Practice which reviews fractions.

Answers for Part 6 of the Home Practice are in the Answer Key at the end of this lesson and at the end of this unit.

Assessment

Students complete the *Fraction Follow-Up* Assessment Pages.

Extension

Assign DPP Challenge V.

---

4. $\frac{2}{3} + \frac{1}{2} = ?$ 5. $\frac{4}{5} - \frac{1}{3} = ?$

6. Roberto's older sister jogs every morning. This morning, after running $\frac{7}{10}$ of a kilometer, she met a friend. She stopped to chat. Then she jogged $\frac{1}{4}$ kilometer more.
   A. Did Roberto's sister jog more or less than 1 kilometer?
   B. Find how far she jogged.

7. Brandon saved $\frac{1}{10}$ of his babysitting earnings in his piggy bank.
   A. What fraction of his earnings did he have left to spend?
   B. Brandon spent $\frac{3}{8}$ more of his earnings on baseball cards. Does he have close to nothing left or close to $\frac{1}{2}$ of his earnings left?
   C. What fraction of Brandon's earnings does he have left?

8. Shannon's mother spends $\frac{1}{3}$ of her monthly salary on rent (which includes heat). Groceries for the month and her car payment add up to about $\frac{2}{3}$ of her salary.
   A. Do these bills account for about $\frac{1}{2}$ of her salary, more than $\frac{1}{2}$ of her salary, or all of her salary (1 whole salary)?
   B. What fraction of her salary is spent after paying for rent, groceries, and her car?

Adding and Subtracting Fractions   SG • Grade 5 • Unit 5 • Lesson 7   **181**

Student Guide - page 181   (Answers on p. 121)

Name _____ Date _____

PART 6 More Work with Fractions
You will need two pieces of dot paper to complete Questions 2 and 3 of this part.

1. Write three equivalent fractions for each of the following fractions.
   A. $\frac{4}{10} = $ ____ = ____ = ____   B. $\frac{2}{3} = $ ____ = ____ = ____

2. Add $\frac{1}{2}$ to each of the following fractions using dot paper rectangles. Label each rectangle.
   A. $\frac{1}{2}$ B. $\frac{1}{3}$ C. $\frac{3}{8}$ D. $\frac{5}{6}$

3. Subtract $\frac{1}{4}$ from each of the following fractions using dot paper rectangles.
   A. $\frac{3}{4}$ B. $\frac{7}{8}$ C. $\frac{1}{3}$ D. $\frac{11}{12}$

4. Write three fractions that are between $\frac{1}{4}$ and $\frac{1}{2}$. ____, ____, ____

5. Write four fractions that are less than $\frac{1}{4}$. ____, ____, ____, ____

PART 7 Solving Problems
Solve the following problems. Choose an appropriate method for each: mental math, paper and pencil, or a calculator. Explain your solutions. Use a separate sheet of paper to show your work.

1. The Yum Yum Deli makes sandwich trays for parties.
   A. Twenty-four sandwiches come on a large tray. If a company orders 27 trays for a party, how many sandwiches are they ordering?
   B. There will be 527 people attending the company party. Can each person have more than one sandwich? Explain.

2. Sturdy paper plates come in packages of 8. How many packages of plates should the Yum Yum Deli supply so that each of the 527 people can have one plate?

3. Of the guests attending, about $\frac{7}{12}$ are working employees. $\frac{1}{8}$ are retired employees. The rest are family members. What fraction of the guests are not employees?

74 DAB • Grade 5 • Unit 5   INVESTIGATING FRACTIONS

Discovery Assignment Book - page 74   (Answers on p. 122)

At a Glance

Math Facts and Daily Practice and Problems

Complete DPP items U and V. Item U reviews units of measure. Item V reviews ratios and can be used as a "problem of the day."

Part 1. Subtracting Fractions

1. Estimate the difference between two fractions. Then use dot paper rectangles to subtract fractions with unlike denominators. Discuss **Questions 1–2** on the *Adding and Subtracting Fractions* Activity Pages in the *Student Guide*.
2. Work in small groups or independently to complete **Questions 3–8**.

Part 2. Using Symbols to Add and Subtract Fractions

1. Discuss **Question 9** in the *Student Guide.* This question leads students through steps for adding $\frac{2}{3}$ and $\frac{3}{4}$ using symbols. Finding equivalent fractions is reviewed from Lesson 4.
2. Discuss **Questions 10–11** in the *Student Guide.*
3. Students complete **Questions 12–18** in the *Student Guide* independently or in small groups. Students compare their solutions. If their answers differ, they determine if the answers are equivalent fractions.

Homework

1. Assign homework **Questions 1–8** in the *Student Guide.*
2. Assign Part 6 of the Home Practice.

Assessment

Students complete the *Fraction Follow-Up* Assessment Pages.

Extension

Assign DPP Challenge V.

Answer Key is on pages 119–123.

Notes:

Fraction Follow-Up

You will need a piece of *Centimeter Dot Paper* for this quiz. Label your work clearly on the dot paper. Follow the No-Diagonal Rule. If a question asks for something that is not possible, say so.

1. For this question, a 4×5 rectangle is one whole. Use your *Centimeter Dot Paper.*

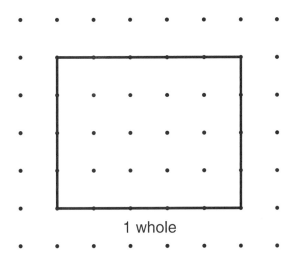

1 whole

   A. Model $\frac{3}{5}$ in two ways.

   B. Model $\frac{2}{3}$ in two ways.

   C. Model $\frac{5}{4}$.

2. For this question a 2×2 rectangle is $\frac{1}{4}$. Use your *Centimeter Dot Paper.*

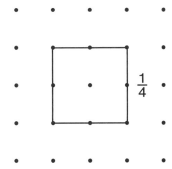

$\frac{1}{4}$

   A. Model one whole.

   B. Model $\frac{3}{4}$.

   C. Model $\frac{3}{5}$.

3. Write number sentences to compare the following fractions. Use $<$, $>$, or $=$ in your sentences.

    A. $\frac{7}{8}, \frac{7}{12}$ **B.** $\frac{5}{6}, \frac{3}{4}$ **C.** $\frac{3}{10}, \frac{2}{3}$

4. Estimate. Is the answer close to 0, $\frac{1}{2}$, or 1? Is it more than one?

    A. $\frac{3}{5} + \frac{4}{9}$ **B.** $\frac{11}{12} - \frac{3}{8}$

5. Add $\frac{3}{4} + \frac{1}{6}$ using dot paper rectangles.

    A. Choose a rectangle to represent one whole. Draw this rectangle on dot paper.

    B. Will you need one or two rectangles to complete the problem? How do you know?

    C. Shade $\frac{3}{4}$ and $\frac{1}{6}$ on your rectangle(s).

    D. Write fractions equivalent to $\frac{3}{4}$ and $\frac{1}{6}$ using a common denominator.

    E. Complete the problem. Write a number sentence to show your answer.

6. Add or subtract. Use any method you choose.

    A. $\frac{1}{2} + \frac{1}{4}$ **B.** $\frac{1}{3} + \frac{4}{5}$ **C.** $\frac{3}{4} - \frac{3}{8}$ **D.** $\frac{11}{12} - \frac{7}{12}$

Student Guide (p. 177)

I. A. $\frac{1}{2}$

B. A 3 × 4 rectangle works since it can be divided into thirds and fourths.

C. First shade $\frac{2}{3}$ of the rectangle. Then erase $\frac{1}{4}$ or $\frac{3}{12}$; $\frac{5}{12}$ is left.

D. Yes, $\frac{5}{12}$ is close to $\frac{1}{2}$.

Student Guide (p. 178)

2. A. $\frac{1}{2}$

B. A 2 × 4 rectangle works since it can be divided into fourths and eighths. First shade $\frac{3}{4}$ or $\frac{6}{8}$; then erase $\frac{3}{8}$; $\frac{3}{8}$ is left.

C. Yes, $\frac{3}{8}$ is close to $\frac{1}{2}$.

For *Questions 3–8* one solution strategy is shown for each. Students might choose other rectangles.

3. Use a 4 × 5 rectangle since it can be divided into fifths and fourths. First shade $\frac{3}{5}$. Then erase $\frac{1}{4}$ or $\frac{5}{20}$; $\frac{7}{20}$ is left.

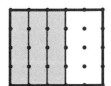 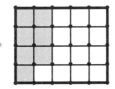

4. Use a 2 × 5 rectangle since it can be divided into tenths and fifths. First shade $\frac{3}{10}$. Then erase $\frac{1}{5}$ or $\frac{2}{10}$; $\frac{1}{10}$ is left.

 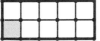

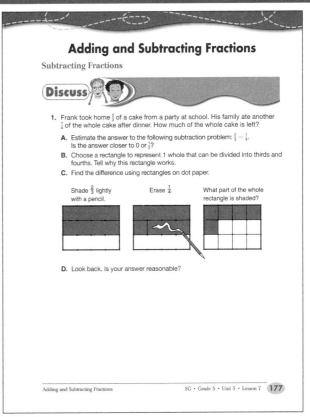

Student Guide - page 177

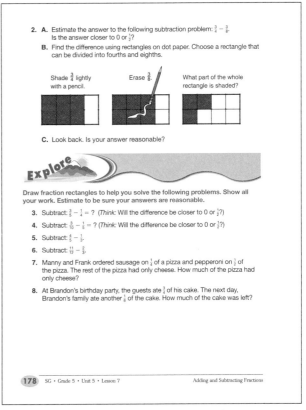

Student Guide - page 178

5. Use a 3×5 rectangle since it can be divided into fifths and thirds. First shade $\frac{4}{5}$. Then erase $\frac{1}{3}$ or $\frac{5}{15}$; $\frac{7}{15}$ is left.

6. Use a 3×4 rectangle since it can be divided into thirds and twelfths. First shade $\frac{11}{12}$. Then erase $\frac{2}{3}$ or $\frac{8}{12}$; $\frac{3}{12}$ is left.

7. Use a 1×4 rectangle since it can be divided into halves and fourths. Shade $\frac{1}{2}$ or $\frac{2}{4}$. Shade $\frac{1}{4}$ too; $\frac{1}{4}$ is left.

8. Use a 3×4 rectangle since it can be divided into fourths and sixths. Shade $\frac{3}{4}$ or $\frac{9}{12}$. Shade $\frac{1}{6}$ or $\frac{2}{12}$ too; $\frac{1}{12}$ is left.

Using Symbols to Add and Subtract Fractions

Discuss

You can use symbols when you add or subtract fractions.

9. **A.** Think about the sum of the following addition problem: $\frac{2}{3} + \frac{3}{4}$. Will it be close to one? Greater than one?

   B. Twelve is a common denominator for $\frac{2}{3}$ and $\frac{3}{4}$. Why? (Think of dot paper rectangles.)

   C. Using 12 as your denominator, write fractions equivalent to $\frac{2}{3}$ and $\frac{3}{4}$.

   D. Then add.

   $$\frac{3}{4} = \frac{?}{12} \qquad \frac{2}{3} = \frac{?}{12}$$
   $$\frac{3 \times 3}{4 \times 3} = \frac{9}{12} \qquad \frac{2 \times 4}{3 \times 4} = \frac{8}{12}$$
   $$\frac{3}{4} + \frac{2}{3} = \frac{9}{12} + \frac{8}{12} = \frac{17}{12}$$

   E. Is the answer reasonable?

10. **A.** Estimate the difference for the following subtraction problem: $\frac{4}{5} - \frac{3}{4}$. Will the difference be closer to 0 or $\frac{1}{2}$?

   B. Twenty is a common denominator for $\frac{4}{5}$ and $\frac{3}{4}$. Why?

   C. Using 20 as your denominator, write fractions equivalent to $\frac{4}{5}$ and $\frac{3}{4}$.

   D. Subtract.

   $$\frac{4}{5} = \frac{?}{20} \qquad \frac{3}{4} = \frac{?}{20}$$
   $$\frac{4 \times 4}{5 \times 4} = \frac{16}{20} \qquad \frac{3 \times 5}{4 \times 5} = \frac{15}{20}$$
   $$\frac{4}{5} - \frac{3}{4} = \frac{16}{20} - \frac{15}{20} = \frac{1}{20}$$

   E. Look back. Is the answer reasonable?

Adding and Subtracting Fractions   SG • Grade 5 • Unit 5 • Lesson 7   **179**

Student Guide - page 179

Student Guide (p. 179)

9. **A.** Greater than one.

   B. Twelfths, 12 can be divided by 3 and 4.

   C. $\frac{2}{3} = \frac{8}{12}, \frac{3}{4} = \frac{9}{12}$

   D. $\frac{8}{12} + \frac{9}{12} = \frac{17}{12}$

   E. Yes, $\frac{17}{12}$ is greater than one.

10. **A.** Close to 0.

   B. Twentieths, 20 can be divided by 4 and 5.

   C. $\frac{4}{5} = \frac{16}{20}, \frac{3}{4} = \frac{15}{20}$

   D. $\frac{16}{20} - \frac{15}{20} = \frac{1}{20}$

   E. Yes, $\frac{1}{20}$ is close to 0.

Student Guide (pp. 180–181)

11. A.–B. Eighths will work; 8 can be divided by 4.

    C. $\frac{1}{4} = \frac{2}{8}$

    D. $\frac{2}{8} + \frac{3}{8} = \frac{5}{8}$

12. A.–B. Eighths will work.

    C. $\frac{1}{2} = \frac{4}{8}$

    D. $\frac{7}{8} - \frac{4}{8} = \frac{3}{8}$

13. A.–B. Sixths will work.

    C. $\frac{2}{3} = \frac{4}{6}$

    D. $\frac{4}{6} + \frac{5}{6} = \frac{9}{6}$

    E. $1\frac{3}{6}$, $1\frac{1}{2}$, or $\frac{3}{2}$

14. A.–B. Tenths will work.

    C. $\frac{2}{5} = \frac{4}{10}$

    D. $\frac{4}{10} + \frac{3}{10} = \frac{7}{10}$

15. $\frac{5}{6} = \frac{10}{12}$; $\frac{1}{4} = \frac{3}{12}$; $\frac{10}{12} - \frac{3}{12} = \frac{7}{12}$

16. $\frac{3}{4} = \frac{9}{12}$; $\frac{5}{12} + \frac{9}{12} = \frac{14}{12}$

17. $\frac{1}{5} = \frac{3}{15}$; $\frac{1}{3} = \frac{5}{15}$

    $\frac{3}{15} + \frac{5}{15} = \frac{8}{15}$

18. $\frac{1}{4} = \frac{2}{8}$; $\frac{5}{8} - \frac{2}{8} = \frac{3}{8}$

Homework

1. $\frac{11}{20}$

2. A. $\frac{2}{12}$ **B.** $\frac{1}{6}$

3. A. $\frac{9}{8}$ **B.** $1\frac{1}{8}$

4. $\frac{7}{6}$ or $1\frac{1}{6}$

5. $\frac{7}{15}$

6. A. less   **B.** $\frac{19}{20}$ of a kilometer

7. A. $\frac{9}{10}$ **B.** about $\frac{1}{2}$ **C.** $\frac{3}{10}$

8. A. More than $\frac{1}{2}$ of her salary.

    B. $\frac{11}{15}$

---

11. A. Add: $\frac{1}{4} + \frac{3}{8}$.

    B. Choose a common denominator for $\frac{1}{4}$ and $\frac{3}{8}$. Eighths will work. Why?

    C. Using 8 as your denominator, write fractions equivalent to $\frac{1}{4}$ and $\frac{3}{8}$.

    D. Add.

12. A. Subtract: $\frac{7}{8} - \frac{1}{2}$.

    B. What is a common denominator for $\frac{7}{8}$ and $\frac{1}{2}$?

    C. Using this denominator, write equivalent fractions for $\frac{7}{8}$ and $\frac{1}{2}$.

    D. Subtract.

13. A. Add: $\frac{2}{3} + \frac{5}{6}$.

    B. What is a common denominator for $\frac{2}{3}$ and $\frac{5}{6}$?

    C. Using this denominator, write equivalent fractions for $\frac{2}{3}$ and $\frac{5}{6}$.

    D. Add.

    E. Look at your answer. Is there another name for this fraction?

14. A. $\frac{2}{5} + \frac{3}{10} = ?$

    B. What is a common denominator for $\frac{2}{5}$ and $\frac{3}{10}$?

    C. Write $\frac{2}{5}$ and $\frac{3}{10}$ with a common denominator.

    D. Add.

15. $\frac{5}{6} - \frac{1}{4} = ?$ **16.** $\frac{5}{12} + \frac{3}{4} = ?$

17. $\frac{1}{5} + \frac{1}{3} = ?$ **18.** $\frac{5}{8} - \frac{1}{4} = ?$

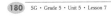
Homework

Complete the following problems. Show your work. Estimate to be sure your answers are reasonable.

1. $\frac{4}{5} - \frac{1}{4} = ?$

2. A. $\frac{11}{12} - \frac{3}{4} = ?$

    B. Look at your answer to Part A. What is another name for this fraction?

3. A. $\frac{5}{8} + \frac{1}{2} = ?$

    B. Look at your answer to Part A. What is another name for this fraction?

Student Guide - page 180

---

4. $\frac{2}{3} + \frac{1}{2} = ?$ **5.** $\frac{4}{5} - \frac{1}{3} = ?$

6. Roberto's older sister jogs every morning. This morning, after running $\frac{7}{10}$ of a kilometer, she met a friend. She stopped to chat. Then she jogged $\frac{1}{4}$ kilometer more.

    A. Did Roberto's sister jog more or less than 1 kilometer?

    B. Find how far she jogged.

7. Brandon saved $\frac{1}{10}$ of his babysitting earnings in his piggy bank.

    A. What fraction of his earnings did he have left to spend?

    B. Brandon spent $\frac{3}{5}$ more of his earnings on baseball cards. Does he have close to nothing left or close to $\frac{1}{3}$ of his earnings left?

    C. What fraction of Brandon's earnings does he have left?

8. Shannon's mother spends $\frac{1}{3}$ of her monthly salary on rent (which includes heat). Groceries for the month and her car payment add up to about $\frac{2}{5}$ of her salary.

    A. Do these bills account for about $\frac{1}{2}$ of her salary, more than $\frac{1}{2}$ of her salary, or all of her salary (1 whole salary)?

    B. What fraction of her salary is spent after paying for rent, groceries, and her car?

Student Guide - page 181

Name _____ Date _____

PART 6 More Work with Fractions

You will need two pieces of dot paper to complete Questions 2 and 3 of this part.

1. Write three equivalent fractions for each of the following fractions.

   A. $\frac{4}{10}$ = _____ = _____ = _____   B. $\frac{2}{3}$ = _____ = _____ = _____

2. Add $\frac{1}{2}$ to each of the following fractions using dot paper rectangles. Label each rectangle.

   A. $\frac{1}{2}$ B. $\frac{1}{3}$ C. $\frac{3}{8}$ D. $\frac{5}{6}$

3. Subtract $\frac{1}{4}$ from each of the following fractions using dot paper rectangles.

   A. $\frac{3}{4}$ B. $\frac{7}{8}$ C. $\frac{1}{3}$ D. $\frac{11}{12}$

4. Write three fractions that are between $\frac{1}{4}$ and $\frac{1}{2}$. _____, _____, _____

5. Write four fractions that are less than $\frac{1}{4}$. _____, _____, _____, _____

PART 7 Solving Problems

Solve the following problems. Choose an appropriate method for each: mental math, paper and pencil, or a calculator. Explain your solutions. Use a separate sheet of paper to show your work.

1. The Yum Yum Deli makes sandwich trays for parties.

   A. Twenty-four sandwiches come on a large tray. If a company orders 27 trays for a party, how many sandwiches are they ordering?

   B. There will be 527 people attending the company party. Can each person have more than one sandwich? Explain.

2. Sturdy paper plates come in packages of 8. How many packages of plates should the Yum Yum Deli supply so that each of the 527 people can have one plate?

3. Of the guests attending, about $\frac{7}{12}$ are working employees. $\frac{1}{6}$ are retired employees. The rest are family members. What fraction of the guests are not employees?

74   DAB • Grade 5 • Unit 5   INVESTIGATING FRACTIONS

Discovery Assignment Book - page 74

Discovery Assignment Book (p. 74)

Home Practice*

Part 6. More Work with Fractions

1. **A.** Fractions will vary. Three possible solutions are: $\frac{2}{5}, \frac{8}{20}, \frac{12}{30}$.

   B. Fractions will vary. Three possible solutions are: $\frac{4}{6}, \frac{6}{9}, \frac{8}{12}$.

   The size of the whole will vary for the dot paper rectangles in *Questions 2–3*.

2. **A.** $\frac{1}{2} + \frac{1}{2} = 1$

   B. $\frac{1}{3} + \frac{1}{2} = \frac{5}{6}$

C. $\frac{3}{8} + \frac{1}{2} = \frac{7}{8}$

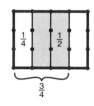

D. $\frac{5}{6} + \frac{1}{2} = \frac{5}{6} + \frac{3}{6} = \frac{8}{6}$

3. **A.** $\frac{3}{4} - \frac{1}{4} = \frac{1}{2}$

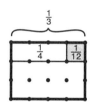

B. $\frac{7}{8} - \frac{1}{4} = \frac{5}{8}$

C. $\frac{1}{3} - \frac{1}{4} = \frac{1}{12}$

D. $\frac{11}{12} - \frac{1}{4} = \frac{8}{12}$

4. Fractions will vary. Three possible solutions are: $\frac{1}{3}, \frac{3}{8},$ and $\frac{3}{7}$.

5. Fractions will vary. Four possible fractions are: $\frac{1}{5}, \frac{1}{6}, \frac{1}{7},$ and $\frac{1}{8}$.

*Answers for all the Home Practice in the *Discovery Assignment Book* are at the end of the unit.

Unit Resource Guide (pp. 117–118)

Fraction Follow-Up

1. A. Answers will vary. The shapes of the fractional parts can vary. The areas must stay the same.

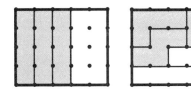

B. It is not possible to divide a 4×5 rectangle into thirds since 20 is not evenly divided by 3.

C.

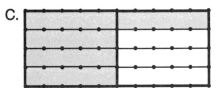

2. A.

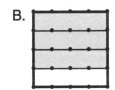

B.

C. It is not possible to divide a 4×4 rectangle into fifths since 16 is not evenly divided by 5.

3. A. $\frac{7}{8} > \frac{7}{12}$ **B.** $\frac{5}{6} > \frac{3}{4}$ **C.** $\frac{3}{10} < \frac{2}{3}$

4. A. about 1

    B. about $\frac{1}{2}$

5. A. A 4×3 rectangle will work since it can be divided into fourths and sixths.

    B. 1 rectangle; $\frac{1}{4} + \frac{3}{4} = 1$ so $\frac{1}{6} + \frac{3}{4}$ will be less than 1.

    C.–D. $\frac{3}{4} = \frac{9}{12}$; $\frac{1}{6} = \frac{2}{12}$

    E. $\frac{9}{12} + \frac{2}{12} = \frac{11}{12}$

6. A. $\frac{3}{4}$ **B.** $\frac{17}{15}$ or $1\frac{2}{15}$

    C. $\frac{3}{8}$ **D.** $\frac{4}{12}$

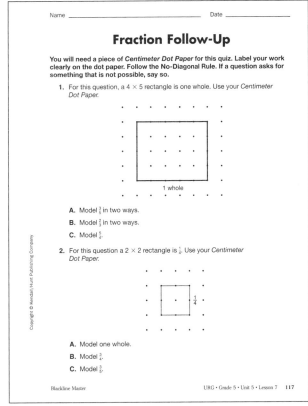

Name _____   **Date** _____

Fraction Follow-Up

You will need a piece of *Centimeter Dot Paper* for this quiz. Label your work clearly on the dot paper. Follow the No-Diagonal Rule. If a question asks for something that is not possible, say so.

1. For this question, a 4×5 rectangle is one whole. Use your *Centimeter Dot Paper*.

1 whole

    A. Model $\frac{3}{5}$ in two ways.

    B. Model $\frac{2}{4}$ in two ways.

    C. Model $\frac{5}{4}$.

2. For this question a 2×2 rectangle is $\frac{1}{4}$. Use your *Centimeter Dot Paper*.

$\frac{1}{4}$

    A. Model one whole.

    B. Model $\frac{3}{4}$.

    C. Model $\frac{3}{8}$.

Blackline Master   URG • Grade 5 • Unit 5 • Lesson 7   **117**

Unit Resource Guide - page 117

Name _____   **Date** _____

3. Write number sentences to compare the following fractions. Use $<$, $>$, or $=$ in your sentences.

    A. $\frac{7}{8}$, $\frac{7}{12}$ **B.** $\frac{5}{6}$, $\frac{3}{4}$ **C.** $\frac{3}{10}$, $\frac{2}{3}$

4. Estimate. Is the answer close to 0, $\frac{1}{2}$, or 1? Is it more than one?

    A. $\frac{3}{5} + \frac{4}{9}$ **B.** $\frac{11}{12} - \frac{3}{8}$

5. Add $\frac{3}{4} + \frac{1}{6}$ using dot paper rectangles.

    A. Choose a rectangle to represent one whole. Draw this rectangle on dot paper.

    B. Will you need one or two rectangles to complete the problem? How do you know?

    C. Shade $\frac{3}{4}$ and $\frac{1}{6}$ on your rectangle(s).

    D. Write fractions equivalent to $\frac{3}{4}$ and $\frac{1}{6}$ using a common denominator.

    E. Complete the problem. Write a number sentence to show your answer.

6. Add or subtract. Use any method you choose.

    A. $\frac{1}{2} + \frac{1}{4}$ **B.** $\frac{1}{3} + \frac{4}{5}$ **C.** $\frac{3}{4} - \frac{3}{8}$ **D.** $\frac{11}{12} - \frac{7}{12}$

118   URG • Grade 5 • Unit 5 • Lesson 7   Blackline Master

Unit Resource Guide - page 118

Shannon's Trip to School

Estimated Class Sessions

1

Lesson Overview

Students solve a variety of problems based on a graph.

Key Content

- Using ratios to solve problems.
- Communicating solutions orally and in writing.
- Translating between graphs and real-world events.

Homework

1. Assign some or all of the problems for homework.
2. Assign Part 7 of the Home Practice.

Assessment

Use any of the problems for assessment.

Materials List

Supplies and Copies

Student	Teacher
Supplies for Each Student • calculator	**Supplies**
Copies	**Copies/Transparencies**

All blackline masters including assessment, transparency, and DPP masters are also on the Teacher Resource CD.

Student Books

Shannon's Trip to School (*Student Guide* Page 182)

Daily Practice and Problems and Home Practice

Home Practice Part 7 (*Discovery Assignment* Book Page 74)

Note: Classrooms whose pacing differs significantly from the suggested pacing of the units should use the Math Facts Calendar in Section 4 of the *Facts Resource Guide* to ensure students receive the complete math facts program.

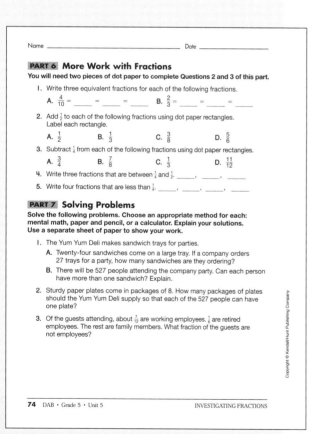

Student Guide - page 182 *(Answers on p. 128)*

Shannon's Trip to School

1. Shannon lives about 1 block from school. The following graph shows Shannon's trip to school one morning.

Shannon's Trip to School

Shannon arrives at school.

Shannon leaves home.

A. How many yards did Shannon travel?

B. How long did it take her to get to school? Give your answer in seconds and then in minutes.

C. How far had she traveled after 1 minute?

D. How far had she traveled after 90 seconds?

E. Did Shannon travel at a constant speed all the way to school? Explain how you know.

2. On her way to school Shannon walked, ran, and stopped to talk to a friend.

A. In what order did she walk, run, and talk to her friend? (What did she do first? What did she do next? What did she do last?)

B. How long did she run?

C. How long did she talk to her friend?

3. Find Shannon's speed in yards per second in the first minute. (*Hint:* Find the ratio of distance in yards to time in seconds.)

Discovery Assignment Book - page 74 *(Answers on p. 128)*

Name _____ Date _____

PART 6 More Work with Fractions

You will need two pieces of dot paper to complete Questions 2 and 3 of this part.

1. Write three equivalent fractions for each of the following fractions.

A. $\frac{4}{10}$ = _____ = _____ = _____   B. $\frac{2}{3}$ = _____ = _____ = _____

2. Add $\frac{1}{2}$ to each of the following fractions using dot paper rectangles. Label each rectangle.

A. $\frac{1}{2}$ B. $\frac{1}{3}$ C. $\frac{3}{8}$ D. $\frac{5}{6}$

3. Subtract $\frac{1}{4}$ from each of the following fractions using dot paper rectangles.

A. $\frac{3}{4}$ B. $\frac{7}{8}$ C. $\frac{1}{3}$ D. $\frac{11}{12}$

4. Write three fractions that are between $\frac{1}{4}$ and $\frac{1}{2}$. _____, _____, _____

5. Write four fractions that are less than $\frac{1}{4}$. _____, _____, _____, _____

PART 7 Solving Problems

Solve the following problems. Choose an appropriate method for each: mental math, paper and pencil, or a calculator. Explain your solutions. Use a separate sheet of paper to show your work.

1. The Yum Yum Deli makes sandwich trays for parties.

A. Twenty-four sandwiches come on a large tray. If a company orders 27 trays for a party, how many sandwiches are they ordering?

B. There will be 527 people attending the company party. Can each person have more than one sandwich? Explain.

2. Sturdy paper plates come in packages of 8. How many packages of plates should the Yum Yum Deli supply so that each of the 527 people can have one plate?

3. Of the guests attending, about $\frac{7}{12}$ are working employees. $\frac{1}{6}$ are retired employees. The rest are family members. What fraction of the guests are not employees?

This problem set is based on the lab *A Day at the Races* (Lesson 5). In the lab, students read and interpret data shown on graphs. This activity reinforces these concepts. You may have students work on the problems independently or in groups to observe their understanding and problem-solving capabilities. Also, you may use some or all of the problems as assessment or homework.

Homework and Practice

- Assign some or all of the problems for homework.
- Assign Part 7 of the Home Practice which includes word problems.

Answers for Part 7 of the Home Practice are in the Answer Key at the end of this lesson and at the end of this unit.

Assessment

Use some or all of the problems as an assessment.

Teaching the Activity

1. Students solve *Questions 1–3* on the *Shannon's Trip to School* Activity Page in the *Student Guide*. They can work individually or in small groups. Have calculators available.
2. Students discuss their solution strategies with the class.

Homework

1. Assign some or all of the problems for homework.
2. Assign Part 7 of the Home Practice.

Assessment

Use any of the problems for assessment.

Answer Key is on page 128.

Notes:

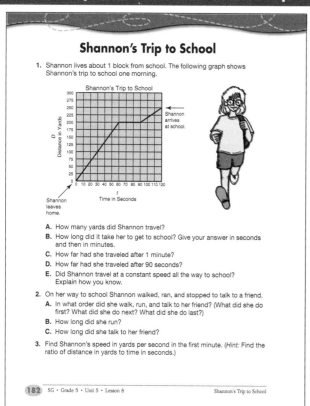

Student Guide - page 182

Student Guide (p. 182)

1. **A.** 250 yards

    B. 120 seconds, 2 minutes

    C. 200 yards

    D. 200 yards

    E. No, the line is not straight, she didn't move at all for 30 seconds.

2. **A.** Shannon first ran, then talked to a friend, then walked.

    B. 60 seconds

    C. 30 seconds

3. $\dfrac{200 \text{ yards}}{60 \text{ seconds}}$

Discovery Assignment Book - page 74

Discovery Assignment Book (p. 74)

Home Practice*

Part 7. Solving Problems

1. **A.** 648 sandwiches

    B. No, only 121 people can have more than one sandwich.

2. 66 packages

3. $\dfrac{3}{12}$ or $\dfrac{1}{4}$ of the guests are not employees.

*Answers for all the Home Practice in the *Discovery Assignment Book* are at the end of the unit.

Discovery Assignment Book (p. 71)

Part 2. Order of Operations

A. 9

B. 2

C. 204

D. 20

E. 120

F. 900

G. 60

H. 90

I. 4

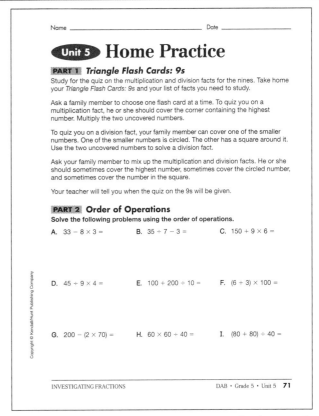

Discovery Assignment Book - page 71

Discovery Assignment Book (p. 72)

Part 3. Ratios

Solution strategies will vary for *Questions 1–5.*

1. Ratios will vary. One possible ratio is $\frac{3 \text{ cm}}{4 \text{ blocks}}$.

2. 3 cm

3. 8 blocks

4. 30 cm

5. 45 cm

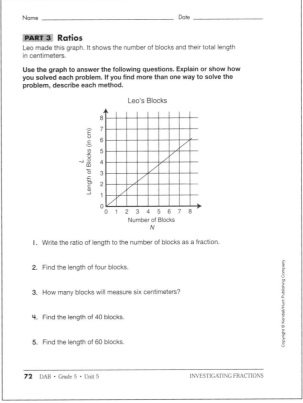

Discovery Assignment Book - page 72

Discovery Assignment Book - page 73

Name _____ Date _____

PART 4 Fractions
You will need *Centimeter Dot Paper* to complete this part.

1. Complete each number sentence. Draw a picture on dot paper for each fraction. A 3 × 4 rectangle is one whole.

   A. $1\frac{2}{3} = \frac{n}{3}$ B. $2\frac{3}{4} = \frac{n}{4}$

   C. $1\frac{1}{6} = \frac{n}{6}$ D. $3\frac{1}{6} = \frac{n}{6}$

2. Write each mixed number as an improper fraction.

   A. $2\frac{3}{5} =$ _____   B. $3\frac{1}{4} =$ _____

   C. $3\frac{3}{10} =$ _____   D. $3\frac{5}{8} =$ _____

3. Write each improper fraction as a mixed number.

   A. $\frac{13}{6} =$ _____   B. $\frac{7}{2} =$ _____

   C. $\frac{10}{3} =$ _____   D. $\frac{14}{5} =$ _____

PART 5 Practicing the Operations

1. Solve the following problems in your head. Estimate the answers to F and G.

   A. 240 + 60 = _____ B. 2089 + 401 = _____ C. 1250 − 300 = _____

   D. 10,000 − 6700 = _____   E. 3800 + 1200 = _____

   F. Estimate: 89 × 18   G. Estimate: 1270 ÷ 50

2. Use a separate sheet of paper. Solve the following problems using a paper-and-pencil method. Estimate to be sure your answers are reasonable.

   A. 473 + 1548 = _____   B. 28 × 59 = _____

   C. 7034 ÷ 9 = _____   D. 3704 − 478 = _____

INVESTIGATING FRACTIONS   DAB • Grade 5 • Unit 5   **73**

Discovery Assignment Book - page 73

Discovery Assignment Book (p. 73)

Part 4. Fractions

Shapes of fractions may vary. Area must be the same as shown.

1. A. $1\frac{2}{3} = \frac{5}{3}$

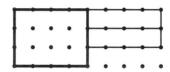

   B. $2\frac{3}{4} = \frac{11}{4}$

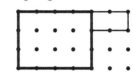

   C. $1\frac{1}{6} = \frac{7}{6}$

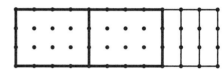

   D. $3\frac{1}{6} = \frac{19}{16}$

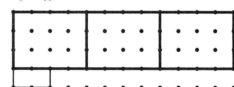

2. A. $\frac{13}{5}$ B. $\frac{13}{4}$

   C. $\frac{33}{10}$ D. $\frac{29}{8}$

3. A. $2\frac{1}{6}$ B. $3\frac{1}{2}$

   C. $3\frac{1}{3}$ D. $2\frac{4}{5}$

Part 5. Practicing the Operations

1. A. 300   B. 2490

   C. 950   D. 3300

   E. 5000

   F. Estimates will vary. One possible estimate is: 90 × 20 = 1800.

   G. Estimates will vary. One possible estimate is: 1250 ÷ 50 = 25.

2. A. 2021   B. 1652

   C. 781 R5   D. 3226

Discovery Assignment Book (p. 74)

Part 6. More Work with Fractions

1. **A.** Fractions will vary. Three possible solutions are: $\frac{2}{5}, \frac{8}{20}, \frac{12}{30}$.

   B. Fractions will vary. Three possible solutions are: $\frac{4}{6}, \frac{6}{9}, \frac{8}{12}$.

The size of the whole will vary for the dot paper rectangles in *Questions 2–3*.

2. **A.** $\frac{1}{2} + \frac{1}{2} = 1$

   B. $\frac{1}{3} + \frac{1}{2} = \frac{5}{6}$

   C. $\frac{3}{8} + \frac{1}{2} = \frac{7}{8}$

   D. $\frac{5}{6} + \frac{1}{2} = \frac{5}{6} + \frac{3}{6} = \frac{8}{6}$

3. **A.** $\frac{3}{4} - \frac{1}{4} = \frac{1}{2}$

   B. $\frac{7}{8} - \frac{1}{4} = \frac{5}{8}$

Discovery Assignment Book - page 74

Name _____ Date _____

PART 6 **More Work with Fractions**
You will need two pieces of dot paper to complete Questions 2 and 3 of this part.

1. Write three equivalent fractions for each of the following fractions.
   A. $\frac{4}{10}$ = _____ = _____ = _____   B. $\frac{2}{3}$ = _____ = _____ = _____

2. Add $\frac{1}{2}$ to each of the following fractions using dot paper rectangles. Label each rectangle.
   A. $\frac{1}{2}$ B. $\frac{1}{3}$ C. $\frac{3}{8}$ D. $\frac{5}{6}$

3. Subtract $\frac{1}{4}$ from each of the following fractions using dot paper rectangles.
   A. $\frac{3}{4}$ B. $\frac{7}{8}$ C. $\frac{1}{3}$ D. $\frac{11}{12}$

4. Write three fractions that are between $\frac{1}{4}$ and $\frac{1}{2}$. _____, _____, _____

5. Write four fractions that are less than $\frac{1}{4}$. _____, _____, _____, _____

PART 7 **Solving Problems**
Solve the following problems. Choose an appropriate method for each: mental math, paper and pencil, or a calculator. Explain your solutions. Use a separate sheet of paper to show your work.

1. The Yum Yum Deli makes sandwich trays for parties.
   A. Twenty-four sandwiches come on a large tray. If a company orders 27 trays for a party, how many sandwiches are they ordering?
   B. There will be 527 people attending the company party. Can each person have more than one sandwich? Explain.

2. Sturdy paper plates come in packages of 8. How many packages of plates should the Yum Yum Deli supply so that each of the 527 people can have one plate?

3. Of the guests attending, about $\frac{7}{12}$ are working employees. $\frac{1}{6}$ are retired employees. The rest are family members. What fraction of the guests are not employees?

C. $\frac{1}{3} - \frac{1}{4} = \frac{1}{12}$

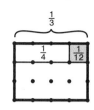

D. $\frac{11}{12} - \frac{1}{4} = \frac{8}{12}$

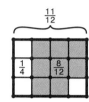

4. Fractions will vary. Three possible solutions are: $\frac{1}{3}$, $\frac{3}{8}$, and $\frac{3}{7}$.

5. Fractions will vary. Four possible fractions are: $\frac{1}{5}$, $\frac{1}{6}$, $\frac{1}{7}$, and $\frac{1}{8}$.

Part 7. Solving Problems

I. **A.** 648 sandwiches

  B. No, only 121 people can have more than one sandwich.

2. 66 packages

3. $\frac{3}{12}$ or $\frac{1}{4}$ of the guests are not employees

Glossary

This glossary provides definitions of key vocabulary terms in the Grade 5 lessons. Locations of key vocabulary terms in the curriculum are included with each definition. Components Key: URG = *Unit Resource Guide* and SG = *Student Guide*.

A

Acute Angle (URG Unit 6; SG Unit 6)
An angle that measures less than 90º.

Acute Triangle (URG Unit 6 & Unit 15; SG Unit 6 & Unit 15)
A triangle that has only acute angles.

All-Partials Multiplication Method (URG Unit 2)
A paper-and-pencil method for solving multiplication problems. Each partial product is recorded on a separate line. (*See also* partial product.)

$$\begin{array}{r} 186 \\ \times\ 3 \\ \hline 18 \\ 240 \\ 300 \\ \hline 558 \end{array}$$

Altitude of a Triangle (URG Unit 15; SG Unit 15)
A line segment from a vertex of a triangle perpendicular to the opposite side or to the line extending the opposite side; also, the length of this line. The altitude is also called the height of the triangle.

Angle (URG Unit 6; SG Unit 6)
The amount of turning or the amount of opening between two rays that have the same endpoint.

Arc (URG Unit 14; SG Unit 14)
Part of a circle between two points. (*See also* circle.)

Area (URG Unit 4 & Unit 15; SG Unit 4 & Unit 15)
A measurement of size. The area of a shape is the amount of space it covers, measured in square units.

Average (URG Unit 1 & Unit 4; SG Unit 1 & Unit 4)
A number that can be used to represent a typical value in a set of data. (*See also* mean, median, and mode.)

Axes (URG Unit 10; SG Unit 10)
Reference lines on a graph. In the Cartesian coordinate system, the axes are two perpendicular lines that meet at the origin. The singular of axes is axis.

B

Base of a Triangle (URG Unit 15; SG Unit 15)
One of the sides of a triangle; also, the length of the side. A perpendicular line drawn from the vertex opposite the base is called the height or altitude of the triangle.

Base of an Exponent (URG Unit 2; SG Unit 2)
When exponents are used, the number being multiplied. In $3^4 = 3 \times 3 \times 3 \times 3 = 81$, the 3 is the base and the 4 is the exponent. The 3 is multiplied by itself 4 times.

Base-Ten Pieces (URG Unit 2; SG Unit 2)
A set of manipulatives used to model our number system as shown in the figure below. Note that a skinny is made of 10 bits, a flat is made of 100 bits, and a pack is made of 1000 bits.

Base-Ten Shorthand (URG Unit 2)
A graphical representation of the base-ten pieces as shown below.

Nickname	Picture	Shorthand
bit		•
skinny		/
flat		
pack		

Benchmarks (SG Unit 7)
Numbers convenient for comparing and ordering numbers, e.g., $0, \frac{1}{2}, 1$ are convenient benchmarks for comparing and ordering fractions.

Best-Fit Line (URG Unit 3; SG Unit 3)
The line that comes closest to the points on a point graph.

Binning Data (URG Unit 8; SG Unit 8)
Placing data from a data set with a large number of values or large range into intervals in order to more easily see patterns in the data.

Bit (URG Unit 2; SG Unit 2)
A cube that measures 1 cm on each edge.
It is the smallest of the base-ten pieces and
is often used to represent 1. (*See also* base-ten pieces.)

C

Cartesian Coordinate System (URG Unit 10;
   SG Unit 10)
A method of locating points on a flat surface by means of an ordered pair of numbers. This method is named after its originator, René Descartes. (*See also* coordinates.)

Categorical Variable (URG Unit 1; SG Unit 1)
Variables with values that are not numbers. (*See also* variable and value.)

Center of a Circle (URG Unit 14; SG Unit 14)
The point such that every point on a circle is the same distance from it. (*See also* circle.)

Centiwheel (URG Unit 7; SG Unit 7)
A circle divided into 100 equal sections used in exploring fractions, decimals, and percents.

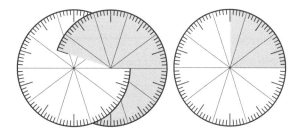

Central Angle (URG Unit 14; SG Unit 14)
An angle whose vertex is at the center of a circle.

Certain Event (URG Unit 7; SG Unit 7)
An event that has a probability of 1 (100%).

Chord (URG Unit 14; SG Unit 14)
A line segment that connects two points on a circle.
(*See also* circle.)

Circle (URG Unit 14; SG Unit 14)
A curve that is made up of all the points that are the same distance from one point, the center.

Circumference (URG Unit 14; SG Unit 14)
The distance around a circle.

Common Denominator (URG Unit 5 & Unit 11;
   SG Unit 5 & Unit 11)
A denominator that is shared by two or more fractions. A common denominator is a common multiple of the denominators of the fractions. 15 is a common denominator of $\frac{2}{3} (= \frac{10}{15})$ and $\frac{4}{5} (= \frac{12}{15})$ since 15 is divisible by both 3 and 5.

Common Fraction (URG Unit 7; SG Unit 7)
Any fraction that is written with a numerator and denominator that are whole numbers. For example, $\frac{3}{4}$ and $\frac{9}{4}$ are both common fractions. (*See also* decimal fraction.)

Commutative Property of Addition (URG Unit 2)
The order of the addends in an addition problem does not matter, e.g., $7 + 3 = 3 + 7$.

Commutative Property of Multiplication (URG Unit 2)
The order of the factors in a multiplication problem does not matter, e.g., $7 \times 3 = 3 \times 7$. (*See also* turn-around facts.)

Compact Method (URG Unit 2)
Another name for what is considered the traditional multiplication algorithm.

$$\begin{array}{r} {}^{2}{}^{1}186 \\ \times\ 3 \\ \hline 558 \end{array}$$

Composite Number (URG Unit 11; SG Unit 11)
A number that has more than two distinct factors. For example, 9 has three factors (1, 3, 9) so it is a composite number.

Concentric Circles (URG Unit 14; SG Unit 14)
Circles that have the same center.

Congruent (URG Unit 6 & Unit 10; SG Unit 6)
Figures that are the same shape and size. Polygons are congruent when corresponding sides have the same length and corresponding angles have the same measure.

Conjecture (URG Unit 11; SG Unit 11)
A statement that has not been proved to be true, nor shown to be false.

Convenient Number (URG Unit 2; SG Unit 2)
A number used in computation that is close enough to give a good estimate, but is also easy to compute with mentally, e.g., 25 and 30 are convenient numbers for 27.

Convex (URG Unit 6)
A shape is convex if for any two points in the shape, the line segment between the points is also inside the shape.

Coordinates (URG Unit 10; SG Unit 10)
An ordered pair of numbers that locates points on a flat surface relative to a pair of coordinate axes. For example, in the ordered pair (4, 5), the first number (coordinate) is the distance from the point to the vertical axis and the second coordinate is the distance from the point to the horizontal axis. (*See also* axes.)

Corresponding Parts (URG Unit 10; SG Unit 10)
Matching parts in two or more figures. In the figure below, Sides AB and A′B′ are corresponding parts.

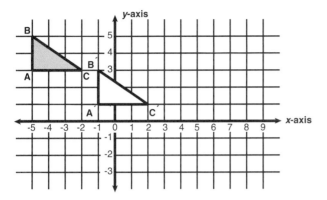

Cryptography (SG Unit 11) The study of secret codes.

Cubic Centimeter (URG Unit 13)
The volume of a cube that is one centimeter long on each edge.

D

Data (SG Unit 1)
Information collected in an experiment or survey.

Decagon (URG Unit 6; SG Unit 6)
A ten-sided, ten-angled polygon.

Decimal (URG Unit 7; SG Unit 7)
1. A number written using the base ten place value system.
2. A number containing a decimal point.

Decimal Fraction (URG Unit 7; SG Unit 7)
A fraction written as a decimal. For example, 0.75 and 0.4 are decimal fractions and $\frac{75}{100}$ and $\frac{4}{10}$ are the equivalent common fractions.

Degree (URG Unit 6; SG Unit 6)
A degree (°) is a unit of measure for angles. There are 360 degrees in a circle.

Denominator (URG Unit 3; SG Unit 3)
The number below the line in a fraction. The denominator indicates the number of equal parts in which the unit whole is divided. For example, the 5 is the denominator in the fraction $\frac{2}{5}$. In this case the unit whole is divided into five equal parts. (*See also* numerator.)

Density (URG Unit 13; SG Unit 13)
The ratio of an object's mass to its volume.

Diagonal (URG Unit 6)
A line segment that connects nonadjacent corners of a polygon.

Diameter (URG Unit 14; SG Unit 14)
1. A line segment that connects two points on a circle and passes through the center.
2. The length of this line segment.

Digit (SG Unit 2)
Any one of the ten symbols 0, 1, 2, 3, 4, 5, 6, 7, 8, 9. The number 37 is made up of the digits 3 and 7.

Dividend (URG Unit 4 & Unit 9; SG Unit 4 & Unit 9)
The number that is divided in a division problem, e.g., 12 is the dividend in 12 ÷ 3 = 4.

Divisor (URG Unit 2, Unit 4, & Unit 9; SG Unit 2, Unit 4, & Unit 9)
In a division problem, the number by which another number is divided. In the problem 12 ÷ 4 = 3, the 4 is the divisor, the 12 is the dividend, and the 3 is the quotient.

Dodecagon (URG Unit 6; SG Unit 6)
A twelve-sided, twelve-angled polygon.

E

Endpoint (URG Unit 6; SG Unit 6)
The point at either end of a line segment or the point at the end of a ray.

Equally Likely (URG Unit 7; SG Unit 7)
When events have the same probability, they are called equally likely.

Equidistant (URG Unit 14)
At the same distance.

Equilateral Triangle (URG Unit 6, Unit 14, & Unit 15)
A triangle that has all three sides equal in length. An equilateral triangle also has three equal angles.

Equivalent Fractions (URG Unit 3; SG Unit 3)
Fractions that have the same value, e.g., $\frac{2}{4} = \frac{1}{2}$.

Estimate (URG Unit 2; SG Unit 2)
1. To find *about* how many (as a verb).
2. A number that is *close to* the desired number (as a noun).

Expanded Form (SG Unit 2)
A way to write numbers that shows the place value of each digit, e.g., 4357 = 4000 + 300 + 50 + 7.

Exponent (URG Unit 2 & Unit 11; SG Unit 2 & Unit 11)
The number of times the base is multiplied by itself. In $3^4 = 3 \times 3 \times 3 \times 3 = 81$, the 3 is the base and the 4 is the exponent. The 3 is multiplied by itself 4 times.

Extrapolation (URG Unit 13; SG Unit 13)
Using patterns in data to make predictions or to estimate values that lie beyond the range of values in the set of data.

F

Fact Families (URG Unit 2; SG Unit 2)
Related math facts, e.g., 3 × 4 = 12, 4 × 3 = 12, 12 ÷ 3 = 4, 12 ÷ 4 = 3.

Factor Tree (URG Unit 11; SG Unit 11)
A diagram that shows the prime factorization of a number.

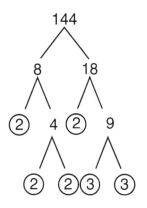

Factors (URG Unit 2 & Unit 11; SG Unit 2 & Unit 11)
1. In a multiplication problem, the numbers that are multiplied together. In the problem $3 \times 4 = 12$, 3 and 4 are the factors.
2. Numbers that divide a number evenly, e.g., 1, 2, 3, 4, 6, and 12 are all the factors of 12.

Fair Game (URG Unit 7; SG Unit 7)
A game in which it is equally likely that any player will win.

Fewest Pieces Rule (URG Unit 2)
Using the least number of base-ten pieces to represent a number. (*See also* base-ten pieces.)

Fixed Variables (URG Unit 4; SG Unit 3 & Unit 4)
Variables in an experiment that are held constant or not changed, in order to find the relationship between the manipulated and responding variables. These variables are often called controlled variables. (*See also* manipulated variable and responding variable.)

Flat (URG Unit 2; SG Unit 2)
A block that measures 1 cm $\times$ 10 cm $\times$ 10 cm. It is one of the base-ten pieces and is often used to represent 100. (*See also* base-ten pieces.)

Flip (URG Unit 10; SG Unit 10)
A motion of the plane in which the plane is reflected over a line so that any point and its image are the same distance from the line.

Forgiving Division Method
  (URG Unit 4; SG Unit 4)
A paper-and-pencil method for division in which successive partial quotients are chosen and subtracted from the dividend, until the remainder is less than the divisor. The sum of the partial quotients is the quotient. For example, $644 \div 7$ can be solved as shown at the right.

Formula (SG Unit 11 & Unit 14)
A number sentence that gives a general rule. A formula for finding the area of a rectangle is Area = length $\times$ width, or $A = l \times w$.

Fraction (URG Unit 7; SG Unit 7)
A number that can be written as a/b where a and b are whole numbers and b is not zero.

G

Googol (URG Unit 2)
A number that is written as a 1 with 100 zeroes after it (10^{100}).

Googolplex (URG Unit 2)
A number that is written as a 1 with a googol of zeroes after it.

H

Height of a Triangle (URG Unit 15; SG Unit 15)
A line segment from a vertex of a triangle perpendicular to the opposite side or to the line extending the opposite side; also, the length of this line. The height is also called the altitude.

Hexagon (URG Unit 6; SG Unit 6)
A six-sided polygon.

Hypotenuse (URG Unit 15; SG Unit 15)
The longest side of a right triangle.

I

Image (URG Unit 10; SG Unit 10)
The result of a transformation, in particular a slide (translation) or a flip (reflection), in a coordinate plane. The new figure after the slide or flip is the image of the old figure.

Impossible Event (URG Unit 7; SG Unit 7)
An event that has a probability of 0 or 0%.

Improper Fraction (URG Unit 3; SG Unit 3)
A fraction in which the numerator is greater than or equal to the denominator. An improper fraction is greater than or equal to one.

Infinite (URG Unit 2)
Never ending, immeasurably great, unlimited.

Interpolation (URG Unit 13; SG Unit 13)
Making predictions or estimating values that lie between data points in a set of data.

Intersect (URG Unit 14)
To meet or cross.

Isosceles Triangle (URG Unit 6 & Unit 15)
A triangle that has at least two sides of equal length.

J

K

L

Lattice Multiplication
(URG Unit 9; SG Unit 9)
A method for multiplying that
uses a lattice to arrange the
partial products so the digits are
correctly placed in the correct
place value columns. A lattice
for 43 × 96 = 4128 is shown at
the right.

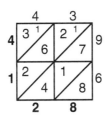

Legs of a Right Triangle (URG Unit 15; SG Unit 15)
The two sides of a right triangle that form the right angle.

Length of a Rectangle (URG Unit 4 & Unit 15;
SG Unit 4 & Unit 15)
The distance along one side of a rectangle.

Line
A set of points that form a straight path extending infi-
nitely in two directions.

Line of Reflection (URG Unit 10)
A line that acts as a mirror so that after a shape is flipped
over the line, corresponding points are at the same distance (equidistant) from the line.

Line Segment (URG Unit 14)
A part of a line between and including two points, called
the endpoints.

Liter (URG Unit 13)
Metric unit used to measure volume. A liter is a little
more than a quart.

Lowest Terms (SG Unit 11)
A fraction is in lowest terms if the numerator and
denominator have no common factor greater than 1.

M

Manipulated Variable (URG Unit 4; SG Unit 4)
In an experiment, the variable with values known at the
beginning of the experiment. The experimenter often
chooses these values before data is collected. The manipulated variable is often called the independent variable.

Mass (URG Unit 13)
The amount of matter in an object.

Mean (URG Unit 1 & Unit 4; SG Unit 1 & Unit 4)
An average of a set of numbers that is found by adding
the values of the data and dividing by the number of
values.

Measurement Division (URG Unit 4)
Division as equal grouping. The total number of objects
and the number of objects in each group are known. The
number of groups is the unknown. For example, tulip
bulbs come in packages of 8. If 216 bulbs are sold, how
many packages are sold?

Median (URG Unit 1; SG Unit 1)
For a set with an odd number of data arranged in order,
it is the middle number. For an even number of data
arranged in order, it is the mean of the two middle
numbers.

Meniscus (URG Unit 13)
The curved surface formed when a liquid creeps up the
side of a container (for example, a graduated cylinder).

Milliliter (ml) (URG Unit 13)
A measure of capacity in the metric system that is the
volume of a cube that is one centimeter long on each
side.

Mixed Number (URG Unit 3; SG Unit 3)
A number that is written as a whole number followed by
a fraction. It is equal to the sum of the whole number and
the fraction.

Mode (URG Unit 1; SG Unit 1)
The most common value in a data set.

Mr. Origin (URG Unit 10; SG Unit 10)
A plastic figure used to represent the origin of a coordinate system and to indicate the directions of the x- and
y- axes. (and possibly the z-axis).

N

N-gon (URG Unit 6; SG Unit 6)
A polygon with N sides.

Negative Number (URG Unit 10; SG Unit 10)
A number less than zero; a number to the left of zero on a
horizontal number line.

Nonagon (URG Unit 6; SG Unit 6)
A nine-sided polygon.

Numerator (URG Unit 3; SG Unit 3)
The number written above the line in a fraction. For
example, the 2 is the numerator in the fraction $\frac{2}{5}$. In this
case, we are interested in two of the five parts. (*See also*
denominator.)

Numerical Expression (URG Unit 4; SG Unit 4)
A combination of numbers and operations, e.g.,
$5 + 8 \div 4$.

Numerical Variable (URG Unit 1; SG Unit 1)
Variables with values that are numbers. (*See also* variable
and value.)

Obtuse Angle (URG Unit 6; SG Unit 6)
An angle that measures more than 90°.

Obtuse Triangle (URG Unit 6 & Unit 15; SG Unit 6 & Unit 15)
A triangle that has an obtuse angle.

Octagon (URG Unit 6; SG Unit 6)
An eight-sided polygon.

Ordered Pair (URG Unit 10; SG Unit 10)
A pair of numbers that gives the coordinates of a point on a grid in relation to the origin. The horizontal coordinate is given first; the vertical coordinate is given second. For example, the ordered pair (5, 3) gives the coordinates of the point that is 5 units to the right of the origin and 3 units up.

Origin (URG Unit 10; SG Unit 10)
The point at which the *x*- and *y*-axes intersect on a coordinate plane. The origin is described by the ordered pair (0, 0) and serves as a reference point so that all the points on the plane can be located by ordered pairs.

P

Pack (URG Unit 2; SG Unit 2)
A cube that measures 10 cm on each edge. It is one of the base-ten pieces and is often used to represent 1000. (*See also* base-ten pieces.)

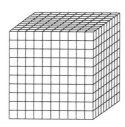

Parallel Lines (URG Unit 6 & Unit 10)
Lines that are in the same direction. In the plane, parallel lines are lines that do not intersect.

Parallelogram (URG Unit 6)
A quadrilateral with two pairs of parallel sides.

Partial Product (URG Unit 2)
One portion of the multiplication process in the all-partials multiplication method, e.g., in the problem 3×186 there are three partial products: $3 \times 6 = \underline{18}$, $3 \times 80 = \underline{240}$, and $3 \times 100 = \underline{300}$. (*See also* all-partials multiplication method.)

Partitive Division (URG Unit 4)
Division as equal sharing. The total number of objects and the number of groups are known. The number of objects in each group is the unknown. For example, Frank has 144 marbles that he divides equally into 6 groups. How many marbles are in each group?

Pentagon (URG Unit 6; SG Unit 6)
A five-sided polygon.

Percent (URG Unit 7; SG Unit 7)
Per hundred or out of 100. A special ratio that compares a number to 100. For example, 20% (twenty percent) of the jelly beans are yellow means that out of every 100 jelly beans, 20 are yellow.

Perimeter (URG Unit 15; SG Unit 15)
The distance around a two-dimensional shape.

Period (SG Unit 2)
A group of three places in a large number, starting on the right, often separated by commas as shown at the right.

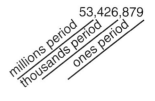

Perpendicular Lines (URG Unit 14 & Unit 15; SG Unit 14)
Lines that meet at right angles.

Pi (π) (URG Unit 14; SG Unit 14)
The ratio of the circumference to diameter of a circle. $\pi = 3.14159265358979. \ldots$ It is a nonterminating, nonrepeating decimal.

Place (SG Unit 2)
The position of a digit in a number.

Place Value (URG Unit 2; SG Unit 2)
The value of a digit in a number. For example, the 5 is in the hundreds place in 4573, so it stands for 500.

Polygon (URG Unit 6; SG Unit 6)
A two-dimensional connected figure made of line segments in which each endpoint of every side meets with an endpoint of exactly one other side.

Population (URG Unit 1 Unit 1)
A collection of persons or things whose properties will be analyzed in a survey or experiment.

Portfolio (URG Unit 2; SG Unit 2)
A collection of student work that show how a student's skills, attitudes, and knowledge change over time.

Positive Number (URG Unit 10; SG Unit 10)
A number greater than zero; a number to the right of zero on a horizontal number line.

Power (URG Unit 2; SG Unit 2)
An exponent. Read 10^4 as, "ten to the fourth power" or "ten to the fourth." We say 10,000 or 10^4 is the fourth power of ten.

Prime Factorization (URG Unit 11; SG Unit 11)
Writing a number as a product of primes. The prime factorization of 100 is $2 \times 2 \times 5 \times 5$.

Prime Number (URG Unit 11; SG Unit 11)
A number that has exactly two factors: itself and 1. For example, 7 has exactly two distinct factors, 1 and 7.

Probability (URG Unit 7; SG Unit 1 & Unit 7)
A number from 0 to 1 (0% to 100%) that describes how likely an event is to happen. The closer that the probability of an event is to one, the more likely the event will happen.

Product (URG Unit 2; SG Unit 2)
The answer to a multiplication problem. In the problem $3 \times 4 = 12$, 12 is the product.

Proper Fraction (URG Unit 3; SG Unit 3)
A fraction in which the numerator is less than the denominator. Proper fractions are less than one.

Proportion (URG Unit 3 & Unit 13; SG Unit 13)
A statement that two ratios are equal.

Protractor (URG Unit 6; SG Unit 6)
A tool for measuring angles.

Q

Quadrants (URG Unit 10; SG Unit 10)
The four sections of a coordinate grid that are separated by the axes.

Quadrilateral (URG Unit 6; SG Unit 6)
A polygon with four sides. (*See also* polygon.)

Quotient (URG Unit 4 & Unit 9; SG Unit 2, Unit 4, & Unit 9)
The answer to a division problem. In the problem $12 \div 3 = 4$, the 4 is the quotient.

R

Radius (URG Unit 14; SG Unit 14)
1. A line segment connecting the center of a circle to any point on the circle.
2. The length of this line segment.

Ratio (URG Unit 3 & Unit 12; SG Unit 3 & Unit 13)
A way to compare two numbers or quantities using division. It is often written as a fraction.

Ray (URG Unit 6; SG Unit 6)
A part of a line with one endpoint that extends indefinitely in one direction.

Rectangle (URG Unit 6; SG Unit 6)
A quadrilateral with four right angles.

Reflection (URG Unit 10)
(*See* flip.)

Regular Polygon (URG Unit 6; SG Unit 6; DAB Unit 6)
A polygon with all sides of equal length and all angles equal.

Remainder (URG Unit 4 & Unit 9; SG Unit 4 & Unit 9)
Something that remains or is left after a division problem. The portion of the dividend that is not evenly divisible by the divisor, e.g., $16 \div 5 = 3$ with 1 as a remainder.

Repeating Decimals (SG Unit 9)
A decimal fraction with one or more digits repeating without end.

Responding Variable (URG Unit 4; SG Unit 4)
The variable whose values result from the experiment. Experimenters find the values of the responding variable by doing the experiment. The responding variable is often called the dependent variable.

Rhombus (URG Unit 6; SG Unit 6)
A quadrilateral with four equal sides.

Right Angle (URG Unit 6; SG Unit 6)
An angle that measures 90°.

Right Triangle (URG Unit 6 & Unit 15; SG Unit 6 & Unit 15)
A triangle that contains a right angle.

Rubric (URG Unit 1)
A scoring guide that can be used to guide or assess student work.

S

Sample (URG Unit 1)
A part or subset of a population.

Scalene Triangle (URG Unit 15)
A triangle that has no sides that are equal in length.

Scientific Notation (URG Unit 2; SG Unit 2)
A way of writing numbers, particularly very large or very small numbers. A number in scientific notation has two factors. The first factor is a number greater than or equal to one and less than ten. The second factor is a power of 10 written with an exponent. For example, 93,000,000 written in scientific notation is 9.3×10^7.

Septagon (URG Unit 6; SG Unit 6)
A seven-sided polygon.

Side-Angle-Side (URG Unit 6 & Unit 14)
A geometric property stating that two triangles having two corresponding sides with the included angle equal are congruent.

Side-Side-Side (URG Unit 6)
A geometric property stating that two triangles having corresponding sides equal are congruent.

Sides of an Angle (URG Unit 6; SG Unit 6)
The sides of an angle are two rays with the same endpoint. (*See also* endpoint and ray.)

Sieve of Eratosthenes (SG Unit 11)
A method for separating prime numbers from nonprime numbers developed by Eratosthenes, an Egyptian librarian, in about 240 BCE.

Similar (URG Unit 6; SG Unit 6)
Similar shapes have the same shape but not necessarily the same size.

Skinny (URG Unit 2; SG Unit 2)
A block that measures 1 cm × 1 cm × 10 cm.
It is one of the base-ten pieces
and is often used to represent 10.
(*See also* base-ten pieces.)

Slide (URG Unit 10; SG Unit 10)
Moving a geometric figure in the plane by moving every point of the figure the same distance in the same direction. Also called translation.

Speed (URG Unit 3 & Unit 5; SG Unit 3 & Unit 5)
The ratio of distance moved to time taken, e.g., 3 miles/1 hour or 3 mph is a speed.

Square (URG Unit 6 & Unit 14; SG Unit 6)
A quadrilateral with four equal sides and four right angles.

Square Centimeter (URG Unit 4; SG Unit 4)
The area of a square that is 1 cm long on each side.

Square Number (URG Unit 11)
A number that is the product of a whole number multiplied by itself. For example, 25 is a square number since $5 \times 5 = 25$. A square number can be represented by a square array with the same number of rows as columns. A square array for 25 has 5 rows of 5 objects in each row or 25 total objects.

Standard Form (SG Unit 2)
The traditional way to write a number, e.g., standard form for three hundred fifty-seven is 357. (*See also* expanded form and word form.)

Standard Units (URG Unit 4)
Internationally or nationally agreed-upon units used in measuring variables, e.g., centimeters and inches are standard units used to measure length and square centimeters and square inches are used to measure area.

Straight Angle (URG Unit 6; SG Unit 6)
An angle that measures 180°.

T

Ten Percent (URG Unit 4; SG Unit 4)
10 out of every hundred or $\frac{1}{10}$.

Tessellation (URG Unit 6 & Unit 10; SG Unit 6)
A pattern made up of one or more repeated shapes that completely covers a surface without any gaps or overlaps.

Translation
(*See* slide.)

Trapezoid (URG Unit 6)
A quadrilateral with exactly one pair of parallel sides.

Triangle (URG Unit 6; SG Unit 6)
A polygon with three sides.

Triangulating (URG Unit 6; SG Unit 6)
Partitioning a polygon into two or more nonoverlapping triangles by drawing diagonals that do not intersect.

Turn-Around Facts (URG Unit 2)
Multiplication facts that have the same factors but in a different order, e.g., $3 \times 4 = 12$ and $4 \times 3 = 12$. (*See also* commutative property of multiplication.)

Twin Primes (URG Unit 11; SG Unit 11)
A pair of prime numbers whose difference is 2. For example, 3 and 5 are twin primes.

U

Unit Ratio (URG Unit 13; SG Unit 13)
A ratio with a denominator of one.

V

Value (URG Unit 1; SG Unit 1)
The possible outcomes of a variable. For example, red, green, and blue are possible values for the variable *color*. Two meters and 1.65 meters are possible values for the variable *length*.

Variable (URG Unit 1; SG Unit 1)
1. An attribute or quantity that changes or varies. (*See also* categorical variable and numerical variable.)
2. A symbol that can stand for a variable.

Variables in Proportion (URG Unit 13; SG Unit 13)
When the ratio of two variables in an experiment is always the same, the variables are in proportion.

Velocity (URG Unit 5; SG Unit 5)
Speed in a given direction. Speed is the ratio of the distance traveled to time taken.

Vertex (URG Unit 6; SG Unit 6)
A common point of two rays or line segments that form an angle.

Volume (URG Unit 13)
The measure of the amount of space occupied by an object.

W

Whole Number
Any of the numbers 0, 1, 2, 3, 4, 5, 6 and so on.

Width of a Rectangle (URG Unit 4 & Unit 15; SG Unit 4 & Unit 15)
The distance along one side of a rectangle is the length and the distance along an adjacent side is the width.

Word Form (SG Unit 2)
A number expressed in words, e.g., the word form for 123 is "one hundred twenty-three." (*See also* expanded form and standard form.)

X

Y

Z